Auto Quiz

How good are you at recognising car badges and mascots, engine parts, racetracks and international number plates? What do you know about driving and the law, the history of racing, motor slang and famous racing drivers? *Auto Quiz* is packed with questions and answers on these topics and dozens more, and will keep car fanatics of all ages busy and happy for hours.

Sandy and Serge Ransford have in the past been the proud owners of an ex-GPO van, a Lotus Elite and a Ginetta G12. They now drive a Mini Cooper, which they race at sprint meetings in their spare time. Sandy is an editor and Serge an architect, and *Auto Quiz* is their first book.

auto quiz

Sandy and Serge Ransford

Illustrated by Terry Dutton
Puzzles by Tony Streek

Beaver Books

First published in 1978 by
The Hamlyn Publishing Group Limited
London · New York · Sydney · Toronto
Astronaut House, Feltham, Middlesex, England
Reprinted 1978

© Copyright Text Sandra and Sergio Ransford 1978
© Copyright Illustrations
The Hamlyn Publishing Group Limited 1978
ISBN 0 600 30364 0

Printed in England by
Hazell Watson & Viney Limited, Aylesbury, Bucks
Set in VIP Times on the Pentamatic System

Contents

Know your car

1 This symbol can be seen inside a car.
  Where is it found, and what is missing from the
  drawing?

2 The average modern car has nineteen or twenty-one
  lights. What are they?

3 What is a toughened glass windscreen?

4 What is a laminated windscreen?

5 Connect the words in the left hand column with those
  in the right to make car components.
  a brake   pump
  b connecting   belt
  c steering   end
  d stub   chain
  e water   plug
  f timing   shaft
  g big   absorber
  h drive   plate
  i piston   bar
  j master   motor
  k spark   shoe
  l fan   arm
  m starter   rod
  n shock   ring
  o anti-roll   cylinder
  p clutch   axle

Seen on the road

1 What does the sign 'heavy plant crossing' mean?

2 How would you recognise a 'sleeping policeman'?

3 What is this and what is it for?

4 What does TIR stand for and where would you see it?

5 What does this arrow mean?

6 If you saw this sign and flashing red lights, where would you be and what would you expect to happen?

7 At a busy town junction you may see traffic lights with a red sign as shown in (a) and a green one as shown in (b). What do they mean?

(a) (b)

8 What would this trailer be transporting?

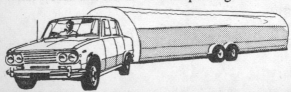

9 When one lorry is being overtaken by another, why does the slower vehicle flash its lights?

10 All these machines may be seen on road construction sites. What are they called?

11 Why is this car 'flying a flag'?

12 What does this sign mean?

RUNNING IN~PLEASE PASS

Heads and tails

These pictures show the 'heads' and 'tails' of some well-known makes of car. Can you identify them?

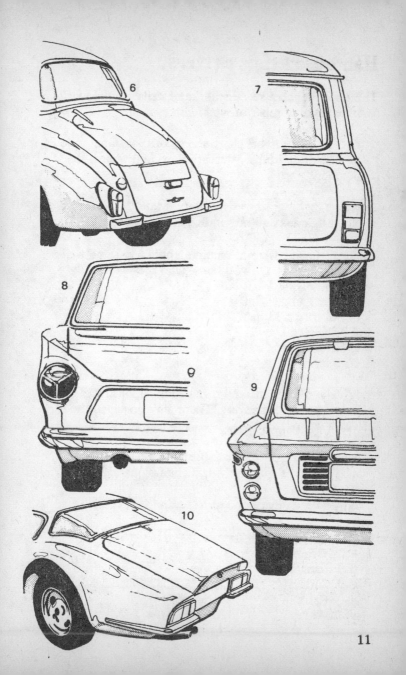

Famous racing drivers

1 Who is the most successful racing driver in the world in terms of number of wins?

2 Two Belgian drivers share the record for the number of wins at Le Mans. Who are they, and what is the number?

3 Which driver tried to win the Le Mans 24-hour race single-handed and only failed in the last hour?

4 The following were nicknames applied to some well-known drivers. Do you know who they were?
   a 'The Flying Mantuan'
   b 'The Pampas Bull'
   c 'Mon Ami Mate'
   d 'The Red Devil'
   e 'Black Jack'
   f 'Superwop'

5 Who won Le Mans and many Indianapolis races but is better known for saying 'There ain't no substitute for cubic inches'?

6 Who was the most successful British racing driver *never* to have won the world championship?

7 Which driver made the most Grand Prix starts?

8 Pair the driver with the car
   a T. Brooks   BRM
   b J. Fangio   Cooper
   c J. Surtees   Eagle
   d J. Clark   Ferrari V12
   e D. Hulme   Hesketh

f	J. Bonnier	Lotus
g	J. Scheckter	Maserati 250F
h	J. Stewart	McLaren
i	D. Gurney	Tyrrell
j	J. Brabham	Vanwall
k	J. Hunt	Wolf

9 E. Junek, M.-T. de Fillipis, L. Lombardi and D. Galica – what is unusual about these Grand Prix drivers?

10 The strange-looking names below are all famous Formula One drivers, but the letters of their names have got muddled up. Can you sort them out?
a KJICCYKXA
b NAJEHTMUS
c ILMDITEENIPORSFAT
d WRSICKTAJATEE
e YESDROCKETCHJ
f DUINAKILA
g BRITBATOVIMROLILA
h PRIDERACKILPLATE
i TIMORDARATINE
j SPENERTONINERO
k CZENAGROLIZAY

11 Who is the odd man out in the following list, and why?
Jack Brabham, Denny Hulme, Chris Amon, John Watson, Bruce McLaren, Alan Jones

Badges and mascots

Each of these drawings represents a car badge or mascot. Do you know what make of car each stands for?

13 14 15
16 17 18
19 20 21
22 23 24
25 26 27
28 29 30

Parts of the engine

Here is a typical British 4-cylinder engine. Can you name each numbered part and give its function?
N.B. You have to turn the picture on its side.

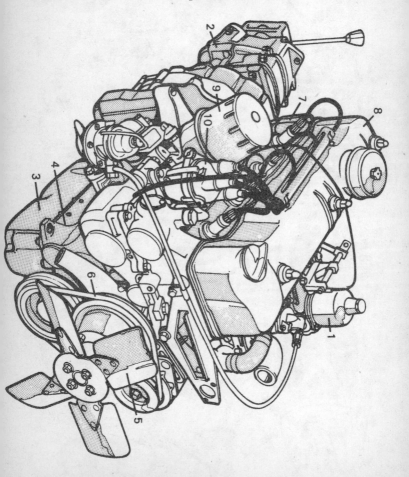

What's missing?

There are at least ten essentials missing from this car. Can you spot them?

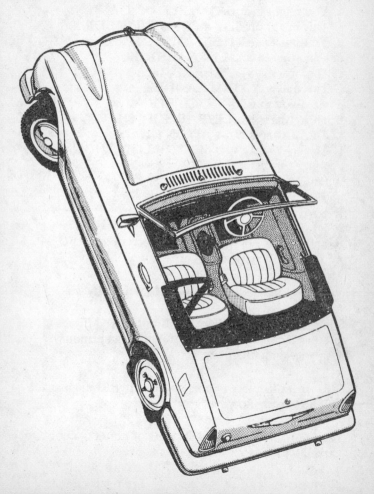

What's in a name?

1 The following are all names of cars produced since
  1945, but they seem to have got strangely mixed up.
  Can you sort them out?
  a You might hear SAY, YELL DR GAVI
  b This might produce a PROD R EFFECT
  c You must use THEIR I PUMP FIRST
  d Can you see SAM IN A MIRROR
  e The order is STAY HERE, LEAP IN SUIT
  f This one is A TRIM LADDER
  g Here you must SPIN ICE ROOM
  h This gives you a LINEAR SUIT SHEEN
  i The answer is NAY, ETON CIDER
  j This may make you SEE YELLOW THORN

2 What connects the following?
  a a ski resort in Italy
  b a city in southern Spain
  c a range of mountains in Germany
  d an island off the coast of Naples
  e a central American country

3 Which car manufacturers 'went to university'?

4 Sunbeam, Jowett, Reliant, Oldsmobile and Pierce all
  produced cars that might be found in an armoury.
  Can you name them?

5 What manufacturer named its cars after Roman roads
  and how many do you know?

6 The following are not inhabitants of London Zoo, but
  cars. Do you know who made them?
  a Tiger   c Impala   e Gazelle
  b Mustang   d Barracuda   f Crested Eagle

g	Sting Ray	j	Hawk	m	Mantis
h	Redwing	k	Bearcat	n	Husky
i	Alpine Eagle	l	Cougar	o	Lynx

7 Which cars were named after the following winds?
  a a light breeze
  b a cold north-east wind in the Mediterranean area of France
  c a north wind in the upper Adriatic
  d a hot south or south-east wind in Egypt
  e a wind that blows in a circular movement
  f a hot wind blowing from the north coast of Africa to Southern Europe

8 Between them, the companies below produced: four 'royal personages', two 'naval gentlemen', two 'officers of ancient Rome', two 'courtly horse soldiers', two old-fashioned 'news announcers' and two 'international representatives'. Do you know what they were? American Motors, Austin, Daimler, Elva, Ford, Mercury, Opel, Triumph, Vauxhall, Wartburg

Behind the wheel

1 On the floor of every car (except an automatic) are three pedals. What is the middle one and which foot operates it?

2 When do you use the choke?

3 What should you check before you start a car?

4 How do you know when to change gear?

5 If the driver of a car you are following does this, what does he mean?

6 What should you always do before changing direction?

7 What is a heeling and toeing
           b double de-clutching?

8 Is it possible to change gear without using the clutch?

9 What three controls have to be carefully co-ordinated when starting uphill?

10 How should you hold the steering wheel?

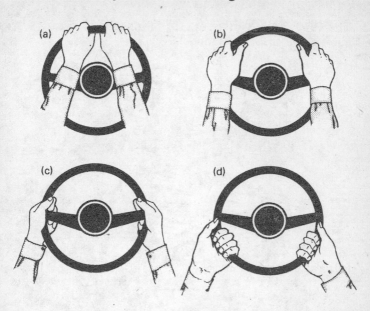

(a)

(b)

(c)

(d)

11 You are driving at 45 mph and want to overtake a lorry. Assuming you have checked that it is safe to do so, what do you do?

12 What would you do if your brakes failed when driving downhill?

13 If you are waiting to turn right and the driver of an oncoming vehicle flashes his lights at you, why do you have to be especially careful?

14 What is aquaplaning and how do you avoid it?

Sports cars of the Fifties

The 1950s was a vintage era for sports cars. Can you name these six famous models?

Road signs and markings

1 What do these signs mean?

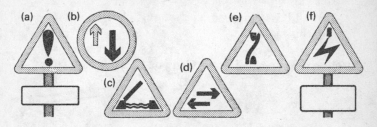

2 There's something strange about these traffic signs. Can you sort them out and say what they mean?

3 What do these road markings mean?

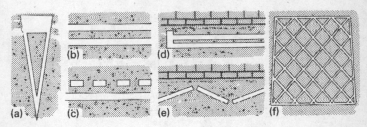

The chassis

1 What is a chassis?

2 Some old cars have an 'underslung' chassis. What does this mean?

3 Here is a typical chassis. Can you identify the marked parts?

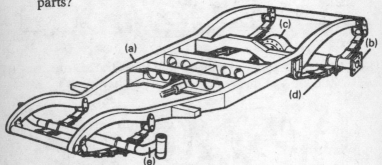

4 What is 'monocoque' or 'unitary' construction?

5 What was the earliest car to use monocoque construction?

6 a Which sports car made between 1958 and 1962 has no chassis and is made from glassfibre?
   b In the 1970s another sports car was constructed in a similar way. It used a Hillman Imp engine. What was it called?

7 What was the 'birdcage' Maserati?

8 a What is a subframe?
   b A number of popular British front-wheel drive cars use subframes. Which ones?

9 What is this? Can you name three British sports cars that use it? (N.B. all are made by the same company.)

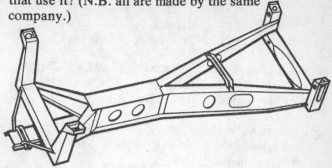

10 What are these?

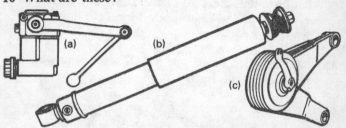

11 a This is sliding pillar front suspension. Which car has always used it?
 b Ford used this type of front suspension for many of their models. What is it called?
 c At which end of a car would you expect to see this assembly?

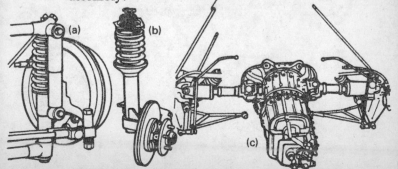

American cars

1 What is the basic difference between the average American car and the average British car?

2 What connects the following cars, and which is the odd man out? Rambler American, Chevrolet Corvair, Chrysler Valiant, Studebaker Lark

3 For which American car did its manufacturers employ four fashion designers to provide special embellishments?

4 What have the following cars in common? Cord 810 roadster, Cadillac Fleetwood Eldorado, Oldsmobile Toronado

5 What were 'Old Scout' and 'Old Steady', and which was the more successful?

6 Here are six American sports cars of different eras. Can you identify them?

(a)

(b)

(c)

(d)

(e)

(f)

Racing formulae

1 What is meant by racing formulae?

2 When did Formula One first come into being?

3 What types of cars were eligible for Formula One racing in the following years – 1950, 1962, 1966?

4 Here are three Formula One cars of the Fifties. Can you name them?

(a)

(b)

(c)

5 Here are four types of American racing car. Which is the odd one out, and why? A. A. R. Eagle, Scarab, Penske, Chaparral

6 Lotus 18, Elva DKW, Stanguellini – what formula did these cars take part in?

7 Who produced a Brazilian Formula One car in 1976, what was it called and who drove it?

8 Here are three 'national' formulae. What are their nationalities and what family cars use the same engines?

a Formula Renault   b Formula Ford 1600   c Formula Supervee

9 Here are three current racing cars, one from Formula One, one from Formula Two and one from Formula Ford. Which is which?

10 Which Formula One racing cars of the Seventies had six wheels, and in what way did they differ from each other?

11 Who built motor cycle rear-engined racing cars, and what formula did these cars dominate?

12 HWM, Alta, Cooper-Bristol, Connaught – what formula did these cars take part in and when?

13 If you saw a racing car like this, what type of racing would it be competing in?

14 What formula uses the same engines that are used in Reliant three-wheeled cars?

15 What is Formula Libre?

Edwardian cars

Here are five typical Edwardian cars. Do you recognise them?

Home towns

Each place in the left hand column is associated with a make of car in the right hand column. Can you link them up?

1	Abingdon	Moskvitch
2	Billancourt	Honda
3	Birmingham	BMW
4	Blackpool	Austin
5	Bologna	Lotus
6	Bradford-on-Avon	Cooper
7	Bristol	Lamborghini
8	Cobham	AC
9	Coventry	Morgan
10	Cowley	Skoda
11	Dagenham	Fiat
12	Derby	Volkswagen
13	Detroit	Maserati
14	Eindhoven	Marcos
15	Göteborg	TVR
16	Hethel	Ferrari
17	Linköping	Jensen
18	Llantwit	Volvo
19	Luton	Reliant
20	Malvern	Porsche
21	Maranello	Saab
22	Milan	Jaguar
23	Modena	Buick
24	Molsheim	Ford
25	Moscow	Invicta
26	Munich	Morris
27	Newport Pagnell	MG
28	Prague	Ginetta
29	Solihull	Rolls Royce
30	Stuttgart	Alfa Romeo
31	Surbiton	Aston Martin
32	Tamworth	Bugatti
33	Thames Ditton	Gilbern
34	Tokyo	Renault
35	Turin	Rover
36	West Bromwich	Vauxhall
37	Witham	Daf
38	Wolfsburg	Bristol

Performance

1 The Bugatti 35B was a favourite of many racing drivers in the late 1920s because of its agility and speed. Was it capable of 65 mph, 90 mph or over 120 mph?

2 What sports racing car of the early 1970s was said to produce 1000 hp?

3 Alfetta 1·6, Volkswagen Golf LS 1·6, Ford Escort 1600 Sport, Renault 16 TX. Here are four family saloons, each with a 1600 cc engine.
   a Which has the top overall speed?
   b Which is the most economical on petrol?

4 How long does it take a modern Formula One racing car to accelerate from standstill to 60 mph? Is it 1·5 seconds, 2·25 seconds, 6·25 seconds or 14·5 seconds?

5 What horsepower was the rear-engined 6-litre Auto Union racing car of 1936 said to produce?

6 Which British GT car of 1961 was claimed to accelerate from 0–100 mph–stop in under 20 seconds?

7 a What is a supercharger? b What is a turbocharger?
   c Which is the more efficient?

8 How long does it take a modern dragster to accelerate from standstill to over 200 mph?

9 Jaguar XJS, Aston Martin V8, Ferrari 308 GTB, Lamborghini Urraco, Maserati Bora, Porsche Turbo, Porsche 928. Here are seven modern Grand Touring cars. Can you put them in order according to their maximum speed, with the fastest first?

The dashboard

Here is the dashboard of a typical family car. Do you know what each labelled part is?

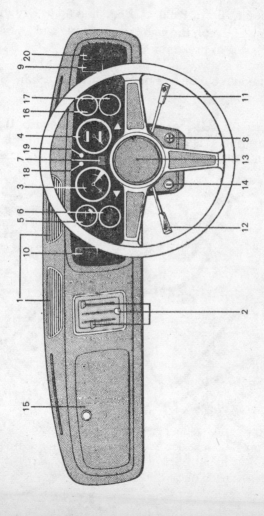

Circuits

1 Where would you be if you were
   a driving down Lavant Straight and heading for Woodcote?
   b swooping down Paddock Bend and up to Druids?
   c doing 150 mph through Abbey Curve and preparing to brake for Woodcote?

2 What famous circuit was built in Surrey in 1906? Who built it, and why?

3 Here are five well-known circuits: A is Monaco, B is Nurburgring, C is Lydden, D is Thruxton and E is Oulton Park. Name the missing straights or bends.

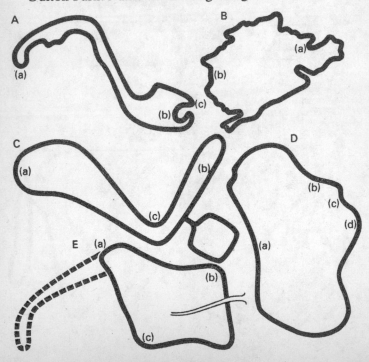

4 What is known as the Brickyard?

5 Where are the following circuits?
   a Riverside
   b Watkins Glen
   c Mosport
   d Kyalami
   e Zolder
   f Daytona
   g Imola
   h Sandown Park
   i Jarama
   j Pau

6 Can you recognise these famous circuits from their shapes?

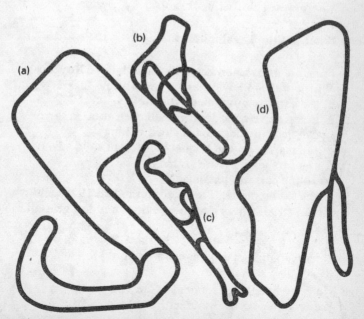

Rolls Royce

1 Rolls and Royce: what were their full names and who was the designer?

2 What sporting achievement first brought Rolls Royce into the public eye?

3 What has been one of the most noticeable characteristics of Rolls Royce cars, right from the first model ever made? (Their names might give you a clue.)

4 Who is reputed to have said, 'You make the cars, I'll sell them'?

5 Rolls Royce are now associated with Derby, but where was their first workshop?

6 What was the Legalimit?

7 There are many legends associated with Rolls Royce cars. Which of the following is true and which is false?
   a the cars are guaranteed for life
   b if you drive a modern Rolls Royce at 60 mph you can hear the dashboard clock ticking
   c the mascot on the bonnet is made of solid silver
   d the cars' engines are sealed
   e all the cars are handmade
   f the 20 hp model, produced in the late 1920s and early 1930s, was made to be driven in top gear all the time
   g after Royce's death in 1933 the RR symbol on the cars' radiators was changed from red to black

8 Here are five famous models. Can you give their names and year of manufacture?

(a)

(b)

(c)

(d)

(e)

Milestones in the development of the car

1 This is an eighteenth-century 'ancestor' of the motor car. What was it called and who made it?

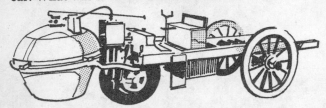

2 What were Infant, Autopsy, Automaton, Era and Enterprise, and what public service did they perform?

3 Here are three early vehicles made by G. Daimler, S. Marcus and K. Benz. Do you know who made each car, and which was the first to be produced?

4 What is Ackermann steering?

5 What car sold at $850 when first produced, then dropped in price to $260, was best driven backwards up hills, was known as a Flivver, and motorised America?

6 These cars were 'milestones' in their country of manufacture, as they were among the first cars cheap enough for ordinary people to buy. But something has gone wrong with these drawings. Can you sort them out and name the cars?

(a)

(b)

(c)

(d)

(e)

Number plates and international registrations

1 Which cars in this country do not have number plates?

2 Where would cars with the following number plates have been registered?

a 1205 EV   e AMN 205H   i RN 2106
b RAF 326H   f BUY 1   j Q 35327
c USA 214R   g J 26295   k PAR 1S
d FOG 1E   h MUS 1C

3 Which countries have these international registration letters?

a CH   d N   g IL   j FL
b CS   e NL   h RA   k E
c GBM   f IRL   i F   l ET

4 What is unusual about these numbers? Do you know where they come from?
a CLV 155   b CDX 410   c CCX 210   d CMV 905

5 What are the international registration letters for these countries?

a Hungary   e Turkey   i Germany
b Iceland   f Jordan   j Austria
c Poland   g Finland   k Greece
d Monaco   h Italy   l U.S.S.R.

6 What vehicles would these numbers belong to?
a 06 GF 46   d 07 RN 19
b 15 AM 34   e 254 LN (printed in red
c 37 GB 82   on a white ground)

7 If your car was registered in August 1967 what would the last letter of its number plate be?

Treasure hunt

Have you ever been on a treasure hunt? Follow the clues in the right order, and 'collect' the letters on the way to find the treasure on the following pages. You may not recognise it immediately!

1 A spire or a tower?

2 The first Elizabeth might have slept here!

3 If you have the right make of car, you can cross here.

4 Leave no stone unturned, blast it!

5 Ruins of Roundheads and Royalists?

6 You might be barred here!

7 No heavyweights this way!

8 Can you stay here if you're no longer young?

9 This way if you're thirsty.

10 Don't pine for too long!

11 If you're lost you can call for help.

12 Are you on the right track?

13 Holiday spot for Boy Scouts?

14 Have you missed the last post?

Now turn to page 106.

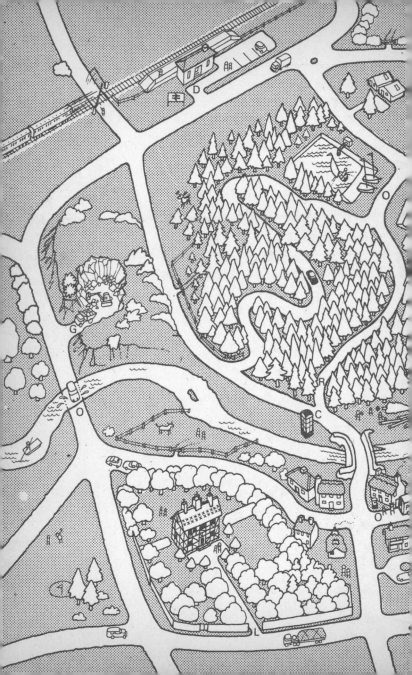

△ HOSTEL

C

K

10 TON

L

F 1642

D

O

start here

Famous designers and their cars

Each of these cars is a typical example of its designer's work, but the designers' names have been put by the wrong cars. Can you sort them out?

1 Ferdinand Porsche

2 Raymond Loewy

3 'Pinin' Farina

4 'Ferry' Porsche

5 Colin Chapman

6 Giorgio Giugiaro

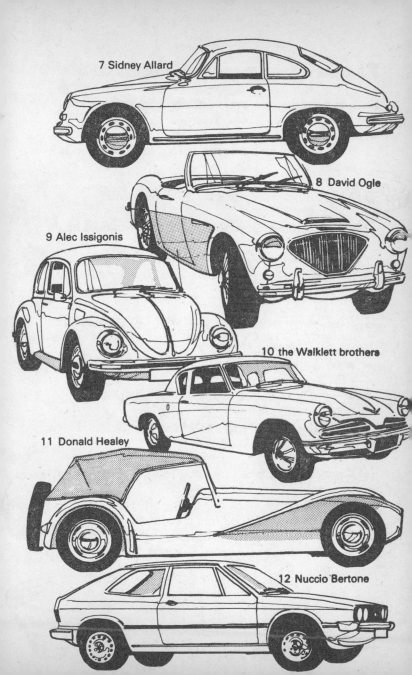

7 Sidney Allard

8 David Ogle

9 Alec Issigonis

10 the Walklett brothers

11 Donald Healey

12 Nuccio Bertone

The dawn of motor racing

1 What was the first-ever motoring competition, and when was it held?

2 What was the first-ever road race, and where was it held?

3 What historic race traversed two continents?

4 Who was James Gordon Bennett, and what did he do for motor racing?

5 What innovation in 1896 made racing cars more comfortable?

6 Where and when was the last 'inter-city' race held, and why were there no more?

7 What were the Prince Henry Tours?

8 What important series of races was held in Sicily?

9 Who was the first Briton to win an international race, and when did he do it?

10 What race took place on Long Island, New York, in 1904?

11 Which of the following cars raced before 1914?
Mors, Peugeot, Lancia, Renault, Fiat, Bentley, Chenard-Walcker, Napier, Salmson, Mercedes

Cars and their engines

Here are six different types of engine, and below is a list of cars. Can you link each car with its engine type?

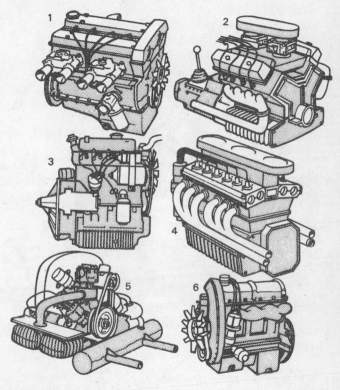

Alfa Romeo Giulia, Austin Allegro, BLMC Mini, Ferrari Daytona, Fiat 124 coupe, Ford Cortina, Ford Escort RS 1800, Ford Fiesta, Jaguar XJS, Lamborghini Miura, Lancia Fulvia, Morris Marina, Porsche 356, Renault 5, Rover 3500, Triumph Stag, Vauxhall Cavalier, Volkswagen 'Beetle'

Cars in fiction

1 In the film *The Yellow Rolls Royce*, how many
owners did the car have and which countries did it
drive in?

2 When did a Mustang chase a Charger round the
streets of San Francisco?

3 This is Herbie. What film was he in?

4 IE EVEN VEG – RAQCARD – A23 – what
connects these three things (the first two are muddled
up)?

5 What car did Steve McQueen drive in the film *Le
Mans?*

6 What does Kojak drive?

7 They weren't Italian jobs that rushed through sewers and flew across rooftops – what were they?

8 In what well-loved book did a motor car cause one of the characters to sit in the middle of the road muttering 'Poop poop', and who was he?

9 What were the Koach and the Drag-U-La?

10 What connects a Bentley Continental, an Aston Martin DB3 and a Lotus Esprit?

11 What is this, and what powers it?

12 What Volvo would you expect to behave in a saintly manner, and why?

Motoring abroad

1 In what European countries is the wearing of seat belts compulsory?

2 What does *priorité à droite* mean?

3 Do you require an International Driving Permit to visit
   a Czechoslovakia
   b Spain
   c East Germany
   d Poland
   e Turkey
   f Luxembourg?

4 What European country requires you to carry a translation of a British driving licence?

5 If you travelled from England to Frankfurt in January, would your watch show the correct time on arrival, assuming you had not altered it since leaving home?

6 If you drove from England to Rome in July, would your watch be showing the right time on arrival?

7 Which country uses yellow headlights, and are they compulsory for visitors?

8 Which mountain pass would you take if you were travelling
   a from Innsbruck to Lake Garda
   b from Grenoble to Turin
   c from Lausanne to Milan (via Brig)
   d from Lausanne to Aosta?

9 Which European countries, apart from the UK, drive on the left?

10 Here are some foreign words and phrases you are likely to come across when motoring in Europe. The first four give warnings, the second four give directions, and the last four are parts of a car. Do you know what they mean and what language they are in?
  a Lavori in corso
  b Nids de poule
  c Höchstgeschwindigkeit
  d Ongeluk
  e Ir para traz
  f Derecha
  g Links
  h Tout droit
  i Scheinwerfer
  j Boîte de vitesse
  k Freno
  l Band

11 For what European country can you buy coupons in Britain to allow you to get cheaper petrol abroad?

12 Which of the following countries drives on the right, and which on the left?
Australia, Canada, Cyprus, Greece, Jamaica, Nigeria, Romania, Sweden, Thailand, Zambia

13 What is 'Australia's own car'?

14 What are East Wind and East Glows?

Famous competition cars

Each of the cars depicted on these pages was highly successful in some form of motor sport. Can you identify them?

Driving and the law

1 In Britain, how old must you be before you can hold a driving licence?

2 What documents must you possess in order to drive a car on a public road?

3 What is the speed limit on a motorway?

4 What is the speed limit on any lighted road unless there is a sign to the contrary?

5 Is it ever permissible to drive through traffic lights at red?

6 When should cars drive with lights?

7 Are learner drivers allowed on motorways?

8 What kinds of vehicles are not allowed to use a motorway?

9 What are you not allowed to do on a clearway?

10 What does a single yellow line along the edge of a road mean?

11 What is an endorsement?

12 What is the 'breathalyser'?

13 When is a driver not allowed to sound his horn?

14 What is an M.O.T. test? What does it cover?

15 What is the standard of eyesight required before you can pass a driving test?

Accessories

Hidden in this picture are seventeen car accessories. How many can you find?

ROAD WORKS

The world championship

1 a When was the drivers' world championship first inaugurated?
  b What category of racing was it based on?
  c Who was the first title holder?

2 Who was the most successful world champion driver?

3 Jackie Stewart was a Grand Prix world champion, but what special record does he hold?

4 Jim Clark, another world champion, held the record for winning the most Grand Prix victories in a year. How many did he win, and in what year?

5 Who was the youngest world champion, and how old was he when he won the title?

6 Who was the oldest driver to win the world championship, and how old was he?

7 How many US world champions have there been, and who were they?

8 One driver won the world championship in a car of his own manufacture.
  a Who was he?
  b When did he do it?
  c What engine did he use?

9 In what car did James Hunt win the world championship? Where and when did he do it?

10 This is a Cooper-Climax F1. Who won the world championship in it?

11 Who is the odd man out in this collection of world champions, and why?
J. Surtees, N. Farina, A. Ascari, M. Hawthorn, P. Hill, N. Lauda

12 Who was the only driver ever to win the 'Triple Crown' i.e. Indianapolis, Le Mans and the world championship?

Three-wheeler cars

Do you know the names of these three-wheelers?

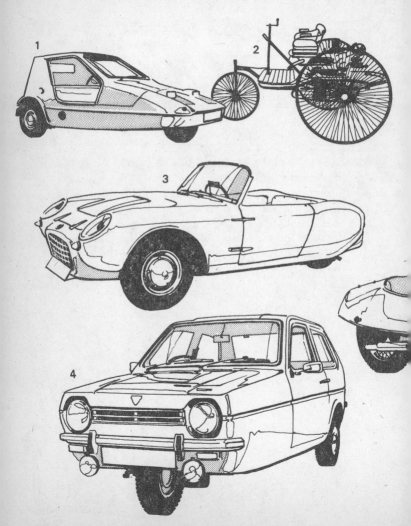

Road tunnels and bridges

1 How long is the world's longest road tunnel? Which countries does it connect?

2 What is the longest road bridge in the UK?

3 What is a Bailey bridge?

4 The world's longest span bridge was nicknamed the 'Coathanger' when it was built. What is its proper name and what does it carry apart from cars?

5 How many bridges cross the Thames between the Houses of Parliament and the Tower of London? Give their names in order.

6 Which of the following cities have a major road tunnel, and what are they called? Bristol, Edinburgh, Glasgow, Liverpool, London, Manchester

7 What is a toll bridge? How many can you name in the UK?

8 What connects a bridge built on floating supports with the number 21?

9 What is the smallest motorway 'tunnel' in the world?

Jargon, abbreviations and slang

1 Do you know what the following car terms mean?
  a coachline   f slicks   k tracking
  b big end   g fastback   l quarter lights
  c torque   h underseal   m re-bore
  d roll   i re-spray   n de-coke
  e drift   j jump leads

2 . . . and the following slang terms?
  a mill   g juice
  b boots   h ton
  c knobblies   i write-off
  d banger   j moth
  e bus   k doing wheelies
  f blower   l burn-out

3 What do these abbreviations stand for?
  a mph   c kph   e mpg
  b rpm   d bhp   f cc

4 If you lived in America these words would be familiar
  to you. Do you know what they mean?
  a hood   g shift
  b trunk   h blacktop
  c gas   i tag
  d muffler   j motor
  e fender   k to nerf
  f windshield

Japanese cars

1 These strange-looking words are the names of
  Japanese car manufacturers with the letters muddled
  up. Can you un-scramble them to find the names?
  a ATOOTY
  b NOHAD
  c ADNUTS
  d BOLUMISTICHIST
  e BUSAUR
  f ZADAM

2 All the cars illustrated here are made by the
  manufacturers listed in question 1, but they have been
  given the wrong captions. Can you give each car its
  correct label and link it with its manufacturer?

(a) Subaru estate 1600

(b) Toyota Crown

(c) Toyota Celica

(d) Colt Mitsubishi Celeste

(e) Mazda 323 hatchback

(f) Honda Accord

(g) Honda Civic

(h) Datsun Cherry

Records

1 What is the highest speed ever attained by a wheeled land vehicle, and who achieved it?

2 What was the first land speed record, who established it and in what year?

3 What did F. Marriott and the Stanley Steamer Rocket do in 1906?

4 Who set the greatest number of land speed records, and how many did he set?

5 Which of the following drivers and cars was
a the first to achieve over 100 mph; b the first to achieve over 150 mph; c the first to achieve over 200 mph; d the first to achieve over 350 mph; e the first to achieve over 400 mph?
drivers: D. Campbell, M. Campbell, J. Cobb, L. Rigolly, H. Segrave;
cars: Bristol-Proteus Bluebird, Gobron-Brillié, Railton-Mobil Special, Sunbeam, Sunbeam 1000 hp

6 What was the first car specially built to break a speed record, and what record did it hold?

7 What was the highest speed ever attained on a public highway? Who attained it, and when?

8 What record-breaking car was buried in sand for forty-two years?

9 What was the original *Spirit of America*, and who drove it?

10 Why was the Mors land speed record of 1902 different from its predecessors?

At the petrol station

1 Why do we have 2-, 3-, 4- and 5-star petrol?

2 What is this and what does it do?

3 What is 'derv'?

4 What is a dipstick used for?

5 Why might you need distilled water?

6 Why might there be a bucket of water and a sponge by the petrol pumps?

7 What is happening here?

8 Why do you need oil?

9 Is oil ever put in the petrol tank?

10 What is a reserve tank?

11 What is happening here?

Vintage cars

Here are ten well-known vintage cars, but they have been given the wrong names. Do you know which is which?

1
1928 4½-litre Bentley

2
1930 Mercedes-Benz
type 770

1929 Bugatti
type 35B

3

4
1929 Alfa Romeo
6-cylinder 'Gran Sport'

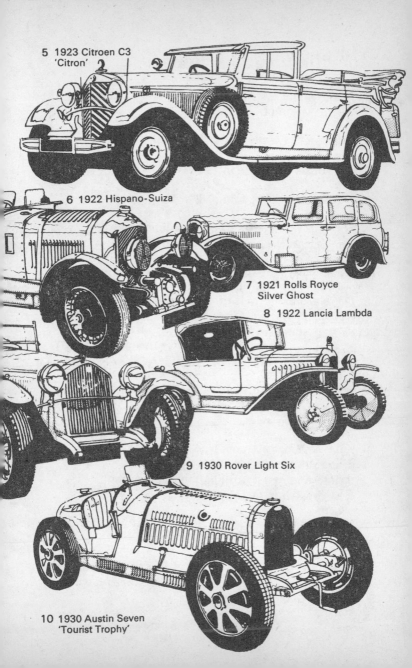

5 1923 Citroen C3 'Citron'

6 1922 Hispano-Suiza

7 1921 Rolls Royce Silver Ghost

8 1922 Lancia Lambda

9 1930 Rover Light Six

10 1930 Austin Seven 'Tourist Trophy'

Motoring organisations

1 Who was the first British sovereign associated with the Royal Automobile Club?

2 What society could you belong to if you owned
   a a car made in 1904
   b a sports car made in 1924?

3 When was the AA founded?

4 Why was the AA patrolman's salute important to its members in the organisation's early days?

5 What society organises the Le Mans 24-hour race?

6 These are the initials of motoring organisations in Europe. What countries do they belong to and what do they stand for?
   a ACI   b AvD   c ACF d RACE e RACB
   f OAMTC g KNAC h ACS i ACP

7 What organisation holds a special driving test for people who have already passed the DOE driving test?

8 What societies are concerned with
   a international motor sport
   b international co-ordination of motoring organisations?

9 What services do the AA and RAC provide for their members?

10 These are the initials of some well-known motor sport clubs in Britain. What do they stand for and what is unusual about the last one?
   BARC, BRSCC, BRDC

Find your way

Modern road planning can make it very difficult to drive directly to your destination. Can you find the shortest route on this map (assuming you are travelling by car and not breaking the law!) from A to B and then to C in under one minute?

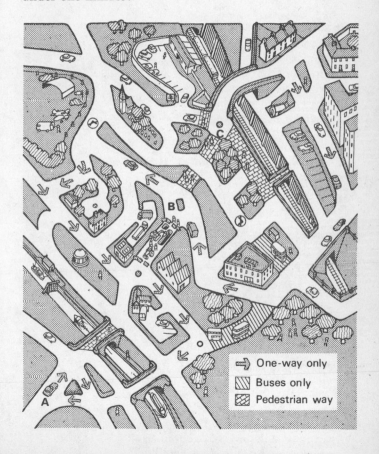

One-way only
Buses only
Pedestrian way

Famous roads

1 What is the Great North Road and what cities does it join?

2 What is the modern name for the Roman Watling Street?

3 In what town or city would you be if you were driving along
   a the Royal Mile
   b Boulevard St Germain
   c Via Appia
   d Park Lane
   e Promenade des Anglais
   f Madeira Drive?

4 Where and what is the Fosse Way?

5 How long is the Pan American Highway and what two points does it connect?

6 Where and what are
   a Scotch Corner
   b Spaghetti Junction
   c the Hogsback?

7 What is the Corniche?

8 In what country would you be if you were travelling on
   a the Road to the Isles
   b the Santa Monica Freeway
   c the Autostrada del Sole?

9 How long is the Alaskan Highway and what was remarkable about its construction?

Veteran cars

Here are five typical veteran cars. Can you identify them?

Club events

1 There are several different types of motor sport. Can you define the following?

   a a handicap   f drag racing
   b a sprint   g a rally
   c a hillclimb   h a sporting car trial
   d autocross   i an auto test
   e rallycross

2 Each of the following drivers is likely to excel in one of the sports mentioned above. Can you connect each driver with his sport?
   John Bevan, Anthony Blight, Rod Chapman, Roger Clark, Roy Lane, Jack Pearce, Dennis Priddle, David Render, Trevor Smith

3 Each of these cars is connected with one of the competitions in question 1. Which car is associated with which event?
   Cannon, Ford Escort RS 1800, Lancia Stratos, Lotus 76, McLaren, Mister Six, MG Midget, Naveb Special, Talbot

When was it made?

These silhouettes show saloon cars which are typical of their time. There is one from the 1920s, one from the 1930s and so on, for every ten years up to the 1970s. Can you give each its correct date?

Rallies

1 Is a rally a race?

2 Where are these rallies held?
   a the Thousand Lakes
   b the Acropolis
   c the Lombard-RAC
   d the Safari

3 What famous rally is always held in early January?

4. If a route card shows signs like these what rally stage is taking place?

5 Who is the only British driver to win the RAC Rally since 1960, and when did he do it?

6 Who won the London-to-Sydney Marathon Rally and in what car?

7 What is a 'Halda'?

8 What is a romer?

9 What is a a special stage
           b a concentration run?

10 Which rally driver is the odd man out – T. Makinen, H. Mikkola, M. Alen, B. Waldegaard, E. Carlstrom, S. Munari, P. Airikkala?

11 What connects the following – Ford Escort, World Cup Rally, Mexico?

12 What rally connects a Sikh garage owner with a Peugeot?

13 What are   **a** black spots
              b quiet zones
              c white roads
              d control points?

14 What are 'yumps'?

15 What make of car attempted to drive from London to Sydney in 1927 and again in 1977?

16 What British sports car made its rally debut in 1976, and what was unusual about it?

17 Which is the odd car out?

(a)

(b)

(c)

(d)

Coachwork

1 Here are nine types of car body and a list of definitions. Can you link the right car with its description?

cabriolet, sports car, saloon, spider/spyder, Gran Turismo, sedanca de ville, coupe, shooting brake, limousine

a a formal, closed four-door car with four to six windows, a division between the driver and passengers and occasional seats in the back

b a large, closed four-door car with (usually) four side windows, a division between driver and passengers and an opening roof in the driver's compartment

c a closed car with a drophead body, large enough to carry four people in comfort. It may have a division between driver and passengers

d a car with van-like lines with a door in the back panel giving access to load space. It has a folding rear seat

e a four- to six-window closed car with seats for four or more people, usually with four doors and openings windows for the driver, intended as family transport

f an open, usually Italian, two-seater sporting car with 'weather-protective' equipment

g a relatively short, two-door car with two or four windows and seats, and a folding hood or solid roof

h a closed version of a sports car

i an open car, usually with two seats but occasionally four, of low build and sleek lines

2 Which is the odd man out in the following list?
quarter light, rearlight, headlight, sidelight

3 Where is a car's waistline?

4 What is a pillarless saloon?

5 What have beetle, duck, boat and fish to do with coachwork?

6 What is a dickey seat?

7 The following are the names of horse-drawn carriages. All except one had a veteran car named after it. Which is the odd one out?
dog-cart, governess-cart, victoria, surrey, buggy, phaeton

Cars around the world

The map on the opposite page shows numbered places in many different countries where cars are manufactured, and beside each number is the name of a make of car. However, the cars are not linked with the right places. Can you sort them out? To help you, the numbered places are named below.

1 Oshawa, Canada
2 Windsor, Ontario, Canada
3 São Paulo, Brazil
4 Cordoba, Argentina
5 Barcelona, Spain
6 Leoben, Austria
7 Lunde, Norway
8 Basle, Switzerland
9 Koprivnice, Czechoslovakia
10 Istanbul, Turkey
11 Haifa, Israel
12 Cairo, Egypt
13 Cape Town, South Africa
14 Port Elizabeth, South Africa
15 Uttarapara, India
16 Shanghai, China
17 T'aipei, Taiwan
18 Taren Point, Sydney, Australia
19 Sydney, Australia
20 Mordialloc, Victoria, Australia

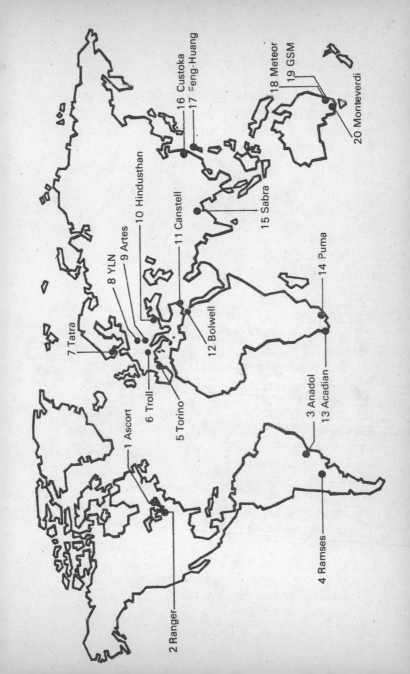

More milestones

1 Ernest Henry designed this engine for Peugeot in 1912. What was it and why was it significant?

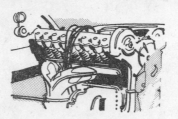

2 What connects these four vehicles?

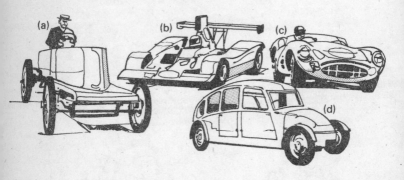

3 Which famous American make was the first to provide an electric self-starter, electric lights, synchromesh gearing and tail fins between the years 1912 and 1948?

4 What manufacturer was the first to mass-produce a vehicle with disc-brakes, self-levelling suspension, a glassfibre roof and a button for a brake pedal? In what year was this done?

5 What make of car had the first mass-produced integral gearbox, transverse engine and independent rubber suspension, sat four people in more comfort than some vehicles twice its length and gave a new word to the English language?

6 What car took the chassis of a mass-produced family saloon, lowered the suspension, replaced the body with a two-seater of wood and fabric and thereby introduced Britain to the ultra-cheap sports car?

7 What is the importance of Multigrade 20/50 oil, and to which car's development was it essential?

8 Why were these two cars milestones of British motoring?

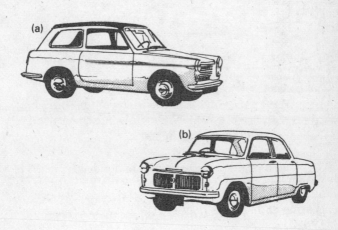

(a)

(b)

Safety

1 Do you know why drivers and front seat passengers
   are advised to wear safety belts? Is it
   a to prevent them getting out of the car too quickly
   b to keep them in their seats in case of an accident
   c to stop them leaning out of the windows?

2 If you came round a corner and saw a red triangle like
   this in the road, would it mean
   a road works
   b that a vehicle had broken down
   c that a traffic sign had blown over?

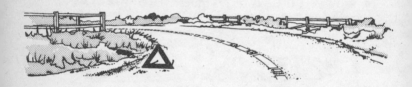

3 From a safety point of view, what are the most
   important components in the following list: gearbox,
   tyres, accelerator, brakes, clutch, windscreen wipers,
   steering, driving mirror, lights?

4 On which of these occasions should a driver 'dip' his
   headlights?
   a when approaching a car from behind
   b when a car is approaching from the opposite
       direction
   c when driving through a built-up area
   d when passing a police station

5 What make of car used to have as its advertising
   slogan 'Safety fast'?

6 If a car skids across the road, should the driver
  a brake
  b steer in the direction of the skid
  c change to a lower gear
  d steer in the opposite direction to the skid
  e accelerate?

7 What is meant by the braking distance? Is it
  a the distance a car must travel before the brakes can be applied
  b the distance over which the brakes are effective
  c the distance it takes a car to stop after the brakes have been applied?

8 Why is it important to know the braking distance? Is it because
  a it tells you how long the brakes will last
  b it tells you how far it takes to stop a car at a given speed
  c it tells you when you can apply the brakes?

9 What are childproof locks?
  a devices to stop children breaking into cars
  b special safety harnesses to keep a child in one place in the car
  c door locks which can be adjusted so they cannot be opened from the inside

Jaguar

1 What connection have the following people with Jaguar cars:
Sir William Lyons, 'Lofty' England, William Heynes, Wally Hassan?

2 What were Grace, Space and Pace?

3 Can you name four open roadster sports Jaguars?

4 Which types of Jaguar won Le Mans and when?

5 You will no doubt recognise this as a Jaguar E-type. When was it first produced and what was its top speed at that time?

6 What were the forerunners of Jaguars (produced by the same company) called?

7 Two types of Jaguar sports car won the first events they entered. Which cars were they and what were the events?

8 What connection is there between the SS100 and a Panther?

9 These are the initials of some of the famous Jaguar racing drivers. Can you give their full names?
a D.H. **b** R.F. **c** I.B. **d** S.M. **e** T.R.
f R.S. **g** M.G. **h** M.H. **i** P.F. - **j** I.I.

10 What connects HWM, Tojeiro and Lister?

11 What was Ecurie Ecosse?

12 What model is this and what is important about its design?

13 How many cylinders does the XK engine have?

14 What engine powers the modern XJS?

15 What essential accessory did Jaguar help to develop?

16 What was the 'Big Cat'?

Engine components

These are all ordinary engine parts drawn from odd angles. What are they?

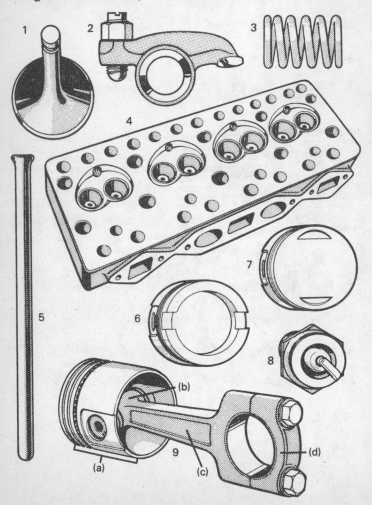

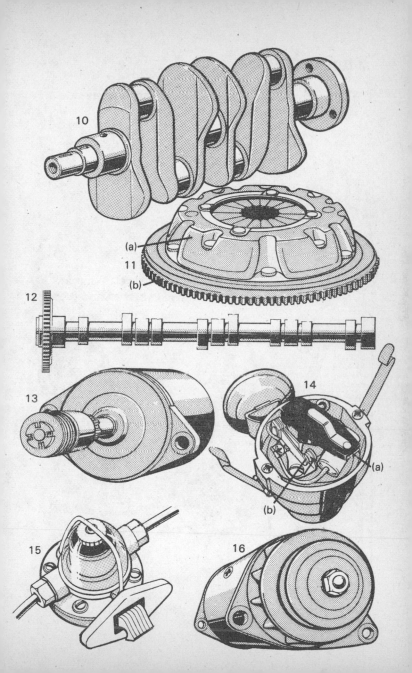

10

11 (a)

(b)

12

13

14 (a)

(b)

15

16

Wheels and tyres

1 This type of wheel was used extensively on cars in Edwardian times. What was it called?

2 Here are some well-known types of wheel. What are they and on what cars would you expect to find them?

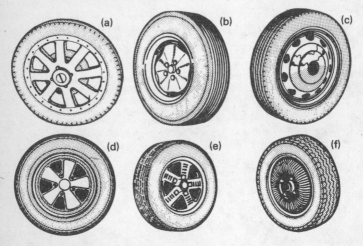

3 Who is Bibendum?

4 What do 'radial' and 'cross-ply' mean?

5 If you fit two radial tyres and two cross-ply tyres to your car, which should go where?

6 In which countries did these makes of tyre originate: Dunlop, Pirelli, Semperit, Kleber, Firestone, Goodyear, Avon, Uniroyal, Michelin?

7 Who produced a NON SKID tyre that had these words as the tread pattern?

8 What tyre firm had the 'groundhog' as its mascot?

9 What are these, and what are they used for?

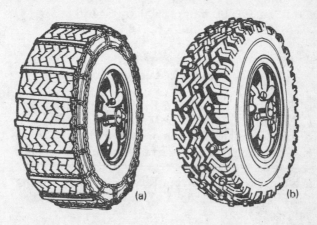

(a)   (b)

10 What are remoulds?

How far is it?

1 Which is nearer to London:
   a Aberdeen or Aberystwyth?
   b Bristol or Bournemouth?
   c Canterbury or Cambridge?
   d Hull or Holyhead?
   e Leeds or Liverpool?
   f Nottingham or Norwich?
   g Sheffield or Shrewsbury?

2 How far is it by road from Land's End to John
   O'Groats? Is it 800 miles (1287 km), 900 miles
   (1448 km), 1000 miles (1609 km), 1150 miles
   (1851 km) or 1500 miles (2414 km)?

3 Which of the paired cities are further apart?
   a Amsterdam and Athens or Barcelona and
     Budapest?
   b Belgrade and Berlin or Brussels and Bucharest?
   c Lisbon and London or Madrid and Milan?
   d Marseilles and Munich or Paris and Prague?
   e Stockholm and Stuttgart or Venice and Vienna?

4 It is quicker to drive from Reading to Bristol along
   the M4 than along the A4, but which route is the
   shorter?

Hatchbacks

Since its introduction a few years ago the hatchback has become very popular. Almost every major manufacturer makes one, and they tend to look much alike. Do you know the names of the models illustrated?

True or false? Absurd facts and fancies

Some of these statements are true and others false. Can you say which is which?

1 In 1901 a man and his wife set out to drive round the world. They covered over 46,000 miles (74,000 km), and where roads were impassable fitted locomotive wheels and drove on railway tracks.

2 A Rolls Royce Camargue costs nearly three times as much as the most expensive Cadillac.

3 The shape of the Volkswagen 'beetle' was influenced by its designer's interest in insects, and the first model to be produced was painted to look like a ladybird.

4 The Coventry Climax engine used in the Lotus Elite was developed from a fire-pump engine.

5 A woman in Wakefield, Yorkshire, failed thirty-nine driving tests in eight years. She passed her fortieth test.

6 In 1955 a Swiss engineer 'drove' a specially prepared vehicle from Putney Embankment to the north bank of the Thames underwater.

7 In 1951 an amphibious jeep 'drove' across the Atlantic.

8 All new cars produced from 1978 onwards must be equipped with rear window wipers.

9 In 1911 a model T Ford made a record descent of Ben Nevis in 2½ hours.

10 In 1933 Morris cars carried miniature 'traffic lights' – green, amber and red – to signal the driver's intended action.

11 To mark the Queen's Silver Jubilee in 1977 a man drove a car up Mount Cook in New Zealand (3764 m) in 7 hours, 25 minutes.

12 A driver in the 1930 Mille Miglia race drove in the dark without headlights so that the leading car would not see him. He overtook to win the race.

13 In 1970 Ford produced a car with five forward and two reverse gears to reduce petrol consumption and make parking easier.

14 In 1970 a man in New Zealand drove a car 109 miles (175 km) in reverse in just over four hours.

You can fuel all of the cars some of the time . . .

1 What three alternatives have been predicted to replace the petrol engine?

2 What fuels other than petrol do some taxis use, and why?

3 What is the connection?

4 This is an electric car. What is special about it, and who ordered a number of them?

5 What is the average mileage an electric car can cover between charges?

6 What have the three cars at the top of the next page in common?

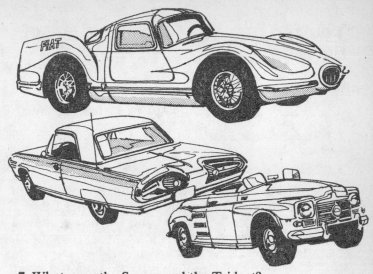

7 What were the Scamp and the Trident?

8 Three racing cars have used gas turbine engines. What were they?

9 This strange-looking vehicle was used in World War II. What fuel did it use, and what is the 'roof-rack'?

10 In 1977 Volvo offered a choice of fuels at the flick of a switch on one of their cars. What were the fuels?

Answers

Page 7 Know your car

1 On the gear lever; the gear positions are missing, thus

2 2 headlights, 2 sidelights, 4 indicator lights, 2 hazard lights, 2 rear lights, 2 reversing lights, 2 interior lights, 1 rear number plate light, 1 boot light, 1 bonnet light, and possibly 2 fog- or spotlights. **3** A screen which, if smashed, breaks into small pieces which cling together to prevent glass from flying about. **4** A screen made from two layers of glass separated by a layer of plastic, so that on impact it does not shatter. **5** (a) Brake shoe; (b) connecting rod; (c) steering arm; (d) stub axle; (e) water pump; (f) timing chain; (g) big end; (h) drive shaft; (i) piston ring; (j) master cylinder; (k) spark plug; (l) fan belt; (m) starter motor; (n) shock absorber; (o) anti-roll bar; (p) clutch plate.

Page 8 Seen on the road

1 Large construction vehicles may be crossing the roadway; this usually happens where a new road is being built. **2** By the bump; they are specially built ridges across a road, usually occurring in a series, designed to slow drivers down. **3** A cattle grid; it acts as a control on the movements of livestock, because while vehicles can drive over it, animals such as sheep, cattle and horses cannot cross it. **4** Transport International Routier; this is seen on the backs of large lorries. **5** Left filter; when the arrow lights up green you may turn left even if the other lights show red. **6** You would be at a level crossing and a train would be approaching. **7** Red means wait, don't cross the road; green means cross with care, unless the light is flashing, when it means wait, don't cross. **8** A glider. **9** To tell the overtaking vehicle that it is safe to return to the inside lane. **10** (a) Bulldozer; (b) hydraulic excavator; (c) motor scraper. **11** To warn other drivers that its load projects beyond the length of the vehicle. **12** The car's engine is new and has to be driven slowly and carefully. The sign lets other drivers know, so that they can safely overtake where possible.

Page 10 Heads and tails

1 Citroen SM Maserati. **2** Fiat 500. **3** Austin Healey Sprite Mk I. **4** Triumph TR5. **5** Austin taxicab. **6** Morris 1000. **7** Mini Mk II. **8** Ford Cortina 1964 model. **9** Hillman Imp (c. 1965). **10** Marcos 1800 GT 1968.

Page 12 Famous racing drivers

1 Richard Lee Petty with 169 NASCAR wins from 1960 to 1975. **2** Jacky Ickx and Olivier Gendebien; 4 wins each. **3** Pierre Levegh, in a Talbot sports car in 1952. **4** (a) Tazio Nuvolari; (b) Froilan Gonzales; (c) Peter Collins; (d) Camille Jenatzy; (e) Jack Brabham; (f) Mario Andretti. **5** A. J. Foyt. He believed that however skilful the driver, a larger engine would always do better than a smaller one. **6** Stirling Moss. **7** Graham Hill; he made 176 out of a possible 184 between 18th May, 1958 and 20th January, 1975. **8** (a) T. Brooks – Vanwall; (b) J. Fangio – Maserati 250F; (c) J. Surtees – Ferrari V12; (d) J. Clark – Lotus; (e) D. Hulme – McLaren; (f) J. Bonnier – BRM; (g) J. Scheckter – Wolf; (h) J. Stewart – Tyrrell; (i) D. Gurney – Eagle; (j) J. Brabham – Cooper; (k) J. Hunt – Hesketh. **9** All are women – unusual in Grand Prix racing! **10** (a) Jacky Ickx; (b) James Hunt; (c) Emerson Fittipaldi; (d) Jackie Stewart; (e) Jody Scheckter; (f) Niki Lauda; (g) Vittorio Brambilla; (h) Patrick Depailler; (i) Mario Andretti; (j) Ronnie Peterson;

(k) Clay Regazzoni. 11 John Watson, because he comes from Belfast. All the others are Australians or New Zealanders.

Page 14 Badges and mascots

1 Bentley. 2 Aston Martin. 3 Alfa Romeo. 4 Rolls Royce. 5 Peugeot. 6 Volkswagen. 7 Ferrari. 8 Maserati. 9 Citroen. 10 Austin. 11 M.G. 12 Vauxhall. 13 Porsche. 14 Alvis. 15 Opel. 16 Morris. 17 Hispano-Suiza. 18 Chevrolet. 19 Mercedes-Benz. 20 Jaguar. 21 Panhard-Levassor. 22 Wolseley. 23 Volvo. 24 Rolls Royce. 25 Chrysler. 26 BMW. 27 Lancia. 28 Lamborghini. 29 Cadillac. 30 Audi.

Page 16 Parts of the engine

1 Carburettor – mixes petrol and air for combustion. 2 Gearbox – converts the power produced by the engine into that which turns the wheels at a rate suited to the speed and pulling requirements of the vehicle. 3 Sump – holds the oil for lubrication. 4 Cylinder block – holds the pistons and crankshaft. 5 Fan – draws air through the radiator to cool the engine. 6 Fan belt – connected to the crankshaft, it drives the dynamo and fan. 7 Cylinder head – holds spark plugs, valves and combustion chambers. 8 Rocker cover – protects the rocker shaft, which operates the valve gear. 9 Oil filter – where the oil for lubrication is cleaned. 10 Distributor – distributes a spark to each spark plug in turn.

Page 17 What's missing?

Windscreen wipers, wheel nuts and hub cap on one wheel, one rear indicator, rear number plate, the air in one tyre, tax disc, gear lever, one safety belt, near-side door, dashboard instruments.

Page 18 What's in a name?

1 (a) Alvis Grey Lady; (b) Ford Prefect; (c) Triumph Spitfire; (d) Morris Marina; (e) Austin Healey Sprite; (f) Daimler Dart; (g) Mini Cooper S; (h) Austin Sheerline; (i) Citroen Dyane; (j) Wolseley Hornet. **2** All are the names of Ford Cars: (a) Cortina; (b) Granada; (c) Taunus; (d) Capri; (e) Mexico. **3** Morris and Austin – Oxford and Cambridge. **4** Sunbeam – Rapier and Stiletto; Jowett – Javelin; Reliant – Scimitar; Oldsmobile – Cutlass; Pierce – Arrow. **5** Lancia; Astura, Aprilia, Augusta, Aurelia, Appia, Ardea, Artena, Fulvia, Flavia, Flaminia. **6** (a) Sunbeam; (b) Ford; (c) Chevrolet; (d) Plymouth; (e) Singer; (f) Alvis; (g) Corvette; (h) Riley; (i) Rolls Royce; (j) Humber/Studebaker; (k) Stutz; (l) Mercury; (m) Marcos; (n) Hillman; (o) Lea Francis. **7** (a) Ford Zephyr; (b) Maserati Mistral; (c) Maserati Bora; (d) Maserati Khamsin; (e) Mercury Cyclone; (f) Volkswagen Scirocco. **8** Austin Princess, Daimler Sovereign, Mercury Marquis, Vauxhall Viscount; Opel Commodore, Opel Admiral; Ford Prefect, Ford Consul; Vauxhall Cavalier, Wartburg Knight; Elva Courier, Triumph Herald; American Motors Ambassador, Opel Diplomat.

Page 20 Behind the wheel

1 The brake; the right foot. **2** When starting the car if the engine is cold. **3** That the handbrake is on, the car is out of gear and the doors are properly closed. **4** By the strained sound of the engine and the fact that the car loses impetus if it is in the wrong gear for its speed. **5** That he intends to slow down or stop. **6** Check with your mirror(s) that it is safe to do so, and signal your intention. **7** (a) Braking with the toe of the right foot while increasing the engine speed with the heel; (b) changing from one gear to another via neutral; this is necessary when the car does not have a synchromesh gearbox. **8** Yes, if the engine is revolving at the right speed. **9** The accelerator, clutch and handbrake.

10 Either (b) or (c). **11** Signal, change to a lower gear, overtake and then pull back in to the correct side of the road as quickly as possible. **12** Put on the handbrake, switch off the ignition, change down progressively through the gears, and if the car still has not stopped, steer gently into the side of the road. **13** Because he could be trying to tell you either that he is letting you through or that he intends to drive past. **14** Skidding caused by a build-up of water between the road surface and the tyres (e.g. in heavy rain). It can be avoided by driving slowly.

Page 22 Sports cars of the Fifties

1 A.C. Ace. **2** Alfa Romeo Spider. **3** Lotus Elite. **4** MG A. **5** Austin Healey 100/6. **6** Triumph TR2.

Page 23 Road signs and markings

1 (a) Danger – the plate indicates what kind of danger; (b) give priority to vehicles from the opposite direction; (c) opening or swing bridge; (d) two-way traffic crossing a one-way street; (e) change to opposite carriageway; (f) overhead electric cable – plate indicates the maximum safe height for vehicles. **2** (a) Give way – the triangle is the wrong way up and the lettering altered; (b) end of restriction – the line should travel upwards from left to right; (c) quayside or river bank – the car should not be in the water; (d) all motor vehicles prohibited – the motor cyclist is facing the wrong way; (e) maximum speed limit – the 40 should be in a circle; (f) level crossing without a gate or barrier – the train is facing the wrong way and the sign should be in a triangle. **3** (a) Give way; (b) stop; (c) no overtaking if doing so means crossing the solid line; (d) no parking; (e) no parking (signifies the approach to a zebra crossing); (f) do not enter the marked area unless your exit is clear.

Page 24 The chassis

1 The base-frame of a car on to which the body, wheels and other mechanical parts are mounted. **2** The axles run above the chassis frame rather than under it (which is more usual). **3** (a) Chassis frame; (b) rear axle; (c) differential; (d) leaf spring; (e) front axle. **4** The car has no separate base frame but is constructed of parts which form the whole body, on to which the suspension, etc., is mounted. **5** Lancia Lambda. **6** (a) Lotus Elite; (b) Clan Crusader. **7** A model built on a chassis constructed from hundreds of short, small diameter tubes which virtually formed the shape of the car. **8** (a) A partial chassis to carry the suspension and engine. It is attached to the car body. (b) British Leyland Minis and 1100 and 1300 saloons. **9** A 'backbone' chassis; Lotus Elan, Lotus Elite 503 and Lotus Esprit use it. **10** (a) A lever arm shock absorber; (b) a telescopic shock absorber; (c) a friction shock absorber. **11** (a) Morgan; (b) Macpherson Strut; (c) the rear; this is an independent rear suspension assembly.

Page 26 American cars

1 The size of the engine: the average American car has a 4-litre engine, the average British car has a 1½-litre engine. **2** They were the first American 'compacts'. The Chevrolet Corvair is the odd man out, as it is the only one that is rear-engined. **3** Lincoln Continental Mk V 1977. **4** All are front-wheel drive. **5** These were Oldsmobile runabouts which competed in the first transcontinental automobile race in 1905. 'Old Scout' was the more successful, winning the 4000-mile race by forty-four days. **6** (a) Cord 812 1935 ; (b) Auburn Roadster 1935; (c) Chevrolet Corvette 1955; (d) Ford Mustang II 1977; (e) Duesenberg Model A 1921; (f) Mercer Raceabout 1911.

Page 28 Racing formulae

1 The classification of racing cars into categories according to their engine capacity, type, weight, design, etc. 2 1948. 3 1950 – cars limited to 1·5 litres supercharged or 4·5 litres unsupercharged; 1962 – cars limited to 1·5 litres unsupercharged – supercharging was not allowed; 1966 – cars limited to 3 litres unsupercharged, 1·5 litres supercharged. 4 (a) Vanwall 1958; (b) BRM type 25; (c) Ferrari Dino 246. 5 Chaparral – it's a sports car and the others are American Formula One cars. 6 Formula Junior. 7 Fittipaldi Bros.; Copersucar; E. Fittipaldi. 8 (a) French, Renault 1600 TS; (b) British, Ford Cortina; (c) German, Volkswagen 'Beetle'. 9 (a) Formula One; (b) Formula Ford; (c) Formula Two. 10 The Tyrrell, which had four wheels at the front, two at the back, and was back-wheel driven; and the March, which had two wheels at the front, four at the back, and was also back-wheel driven. 11 Charles and John Cooper; Formula Three in the late 1940s and mid 1950s. 12 Formula Two, 1950s. 13 Clubman's Formula. 14 Formula 750. 15 A category of race in which all types of cars are allowed to compete.

Page 30 Edwardian cars

1 'Prince Henry' Vauxhall 1914. 2 Daimler 30 h.p. 1913. 3 Renault Grand Prix 1907. 4 Cadillac 1914. 5 Ford Model T 1909.

Page 31 Home towns

1 Abingdon – M.G. 2 Billancourt – Renault. 3 Birmingham – Austin. 4 Blackpool – TVR. 5 Bologna – Lamborghini. 6 Bradford-on-Avon – Marcos. 7 Bristol – Bristol. 8 Cobham – Invicta. 9 Coventry – Jaguar. 10 Cowley – Morris. 11 Dagenham – Ford. 12 Derby – Rolls Royce. 13 Detroit – Buick. 14 Eindhoven – Daf. 15 Göteborg – Volvo.

16 Hethel – Lotus. 17 Linköping – Saab. 18 Llantwit – Gilbern. 19 Luton – Vauxhall. 20 Malvern – Morgan. 21 Maranello – Ferrari. 22 Milan – Alfa Romeo. 23 Modena – Maserati. 24 Molsheim – Bugatti. 25 Moscow – Moskvitch. 26 Munich – BMW. 27 Newport Pagnell – Aston Martin. 28 Prague – Skoda. 29 Solihull – Rover. 30 Stuttgart – Porsche. 31 Surbiton – Cooper. 32 Tamworth – Reliant. 33 Thames Ditton – A.C. 34 Tokyo – Honda. 35 Turin – Fiat. 36 West Bromwich – Jensen. 37 Witham – Ginetta. 38 Wolfsburg – Volkswagen.

Page 32 Performance

1 Over 120 mph. 2 Porsche Can-Am 917 turbocharged. 3 (a) Renault 16 TX, with 104 mph. (b) Ford Escort 1600 Sport, with 34·3 mpg. 4 2·25 seconds. 5 520 hp. 6 Aston Martin DB4 GT. 7 They are both methods of increasing the power of a car by increasing the pressure at which the petrol and air mixture is injected into the engine. (a) does this by means of a device driven directly by the engine, (b) by means of a turbine driven by the exhaust gases. The turbocharger is the more efficient. 8 6·25 seconds. 9 Maserati Bora – 162 mph; Ferrari 308 GTB – 154 mph; Jaguar XJS and Porsche Turbo – 153 mph; Aston Martin V8 – 148 mph; Lamborghini Urraco and Porsche 928 – 143 mph.

Page 33 The dashboard

1 Air vents. 2 Heater and fresh air control levers. 3 Rev. counter. 4 Speedometer. 5 Fuel gauge. 6 Ammeter. 7 Headlamp full beam warning light. 8 Choke operating knob. 9 Windscreen wiper switch. 10 Hazard warning light switch. 11 Indicator switch. 12 Dipswitch. 13 Horn. 14 Ignition switch and steering lock. 15 Glove locker. 16 Oil pressure gauge. 17 Temperature gauge. 18 Ignition warning light. 19 Oil warning light. 20 Windscreen washers.

Page 34 Circuits

1 (a) Goodwood; (b) Brands Hatch; (c) Silverstone.
2 Brooklands, built by H. F. Locke-King to give British cars the opportunity to go at unlimited speeds so they could compete better with foreign cars. 3 A (a) Gasworks Hairpin; (b) Station Hairpin; (c) Mirabeau. B (a) Karussel; (b) Flugplatz. C (a) Pilgrims; (b) Hairy Hill; (c) Devil's Elbow. D (a) Brooklands; (b) Campbell; (c) Cobb; (d) Segrave. E (a) Knicker Brook; (b) Druids Corner; (c) Old Hall Corner. 4 The Indianapolis circuit. 5 (a) Near Los Angeles, USA; (b) New York State, USA; (c) Ontario, Canada; (d) near Johannesburg, South Africa; (e) Zolder, Belgium; (f) Daytona Beach, Florida, USA; (g) near Bologna, Italy; (h) Melbourne, Australia; (i) near Madrid, Spain; (j) Pau, near Lourdes, in SW France. 6 (a) Brands Hatch; (b) Monza; (c) Paul Ricard; (d) Donington Park.

Page 36 Rolls Royce

1 Charles Stuart Rolls, Frederick Henry Royce; the latter was the designer. 2 A Rolls Royce came second in the 1905 Tourist Trophy with Percy Northey driving. 3 Their comparative silence. 4 Charles Rolls to Henry Royce. 5 Cooke Street, Manchester. 6 A Rolls Royce of 1905/1906 specially designed to be incapable of breaking the speed limit of 20 mph. 7 (a) False; (b) true, if sitting in the front; (c) false; (d) false; (e) false; (f) false, though people thought that it was and did so! (g) true. 8 (a) 1907 40/50 Silver Ghost; (b) 1952 Silver Dawn; (c) Camargue 1976; (d) Phantom II Coupe 1929; (e) 1969 Silver Shadow.

Page 38 Milestones in the development of the car

1 The Cugnot steam wagon, produced by Nicolas Joseph Cugnot. 2 Steam-powered coaches, run in Britain in 1834 by Walter Hancock as a public road transport service. 3 (a)

S. Marcus; (b) G. Daimler; (c) K. Benz. Marcus's car was the first to be produced. **4** A system by which each front wheel turns on its own pivot or kingpin, unlike carriage wheels whose axles turned on a single centre pivot. **5** The Ford Model T. **6** The fronts of the cars are not matched with the backs. (a) has a Volkswagen 'Beetle' front and a Morris Minor back; (b) has a Citroen 2CV front and a Fiat 500 back; (c) has an Austin Seven front and a Citroen 2CV back; (d) has a Fiat 500 front and a Volkswagen 'Beetle' back; and (e) has a Morris Minor front and an Austin Seven back. The five cars are therefore: Austin Seven, Citroen 2CV, Fiat 500, Morris Minor and Volkswagen 'Beetle'.

Page 40 Number plates and international registrations

1 Those personally owned by H. M. the Queen. **2** (a) Essex; (b) Cornwall; (c) Aberdeen; (d) Birmingham; (e) nowhere – the letters MN were not issued because of confusion with Isle of Man registrations; (f) Worcestershire; (g) Jersey; (h) Glasgow; (i) Preston; (j) temporarily in Great Britain; Q prefixes are used for cars visiting this country which have either no number plates or those that cannot be understood, and for cars bought in this country for export; (k) Hertfordshire. **3** (a) Switzerland; (b) Czechoslovakia; (c) Isle of Man; (d) Norway; (e) Holland; (f) Eire; (g) Israel; (h) Argentina; (i) France; (j) Liechtenstein; (k) Spain; (l) Egypt. **4** The letters are the Roman numeral equivalents of the digits. (a) is a Liverpool registration; (b) is an Ipswich registration; (c) is a Huddersfield registration; (d) is a Greater London registration. **5** (a) H; (b) IS; (c) PL; (d) MC; (e) TR; (f) HKJ; (g) SF; (h) I; (i) D; (j) A; (k) GR; (l) SU. **6** (a) One belonging to the British Army; (b) one belonging to the Royal Air Force; (c) one belonging to the British Army; (d) one belonging to the Royal Navy; (e) a vehicle carrying trade plates, i.e. an unregistered vehicle which is only allowed on the road if it carries these special plates. **7** F, because E was used from January to July 1967 only.

Page 41 Treasure hunt

1 Church; 2 Tudor house; 3 Ford; 4 Quarry; 5 Ruined castle, dated 1642; 6 Public house; 7 10-ton bridge; 8 Youth hostel; 9 Reservoir; 10 Shorter road through the pine wood; 11 Telephone box; 12 The station; 13 Camp site; 14 Post office. Your letters should be DLOGFOKCORCDLO. Read them backwards to find the treasure.

Page 44 Famous designers and their cars

1 The Walklett brothers – Ginetta G15. 2 Sidney Allard – Allard J2. 3 David Ogle – Reliant Scimitar. 4 Nuccio Bertone – Alfa Romeo Giulia Sprint. 5 Alec Issigonis – BMC Mini. 6 'Pinin' Farina – 250 GT Ferrari. 7 'Ferry' Porsche – Porsche 356. 8 Donald Healey – Austin Healey 100-4. 9 Ferdinand Porsche – Volkswagen 'Beetle'. 10 Raymond Loewy – Studebaker Hawk. 11 Colin Chapman – Lotus Seven. 12 Giorgio Giugiaro – VW Scirocco.

Page 46 The dawn of motor racing

1 A reliability trial, Paris–Rouen, sponsored by the Paris newspaper *Le Petit Journal* and held in 1894. 2 The Paris–Bordeaux–Paris race held in France in 1895. 3 The Paris–Peking. 4 Proprietor of the *New York Herald*, he sponsored the first international series of races, the first one of which was held in 1900. 5 The introduction of pneumatic tyres, first used on a Peugeot in the Paris–Marseilles race of 1896. 6 Paris–Madrid in 1903. It was halted by the French government at Bordeaux after a number of bad accidents and no more races of this type were allowed. 7 A series of reliability trials, held between 1908 and 1911 and inaugurated by Prince Henry of Prussia. The 1910 competition greatly influenced the development of the sports car. 8 The Targa Florio. 9 S. F. Edge, driving a Napier in the 1902 J. Gordon

Bennett race. **10** The first Vanderbilt Cup race. **11** All except the Bentley and the Salmson.

Page 47 Cars and their engines

1 4-cylinder twin overhead camshaft – Ford Escort RS 1800, Alfa Romeo Giulia, Fiat 124 coupe. **2** V8 – Triumph Stag, Rover 3500. **3** 4-cylinder transverse – BLMC Mini, Ford Fiesta, Austin Allegro. **4** V12 4-overhead camshaft – Ferrari Daytona, Jaguar XJS, Lamborghini Miura. **5** Flat 4 – Lancia Fulvia, Porsche 356, Volkswagen 'Beetle'. **6** 4-cylinder 'in line' – Ford Cortina, Morris Marina, Renault 5, Vauxhall Cavalier.

Page 48 Cars in fiction

1 Three; England, Italy and Yugoslavia. **2** In the film *Bullitt* a 390 GT Mustang chases a Dodge Charger. **3** *The Love Bug*. **4** The film *Genevieve* (the first word). The car was a Darracq (the second word) and it drove in the London-to-Brighton Veteran Car Run, down the A23. **5** A 600 hp Porsche 917. **6** A Buick. **7** Mini-Coopers – in *The Italian Job*. **8** Kenneth Grahame's *The Wind in the Willows*; Toad. **9** Vehicles used in the TV series *The Munsters*. **10** They are all cars driven by James Bond, the first two in the books and the last in the latest film, *The Spy Who Loved Me*. **11** Batman's Batmobile, powered by a 7-litre Ford Thunderbird V-8 engine. **12** The Volvo P 1800 S, because it was driven by Simon Templar (The Saint) in the television series based on Leslie Charteris's books.

Page 50 Motoring abroad

1 Belgium, Luxembourg, the Netherlands, Switzerland, plus France and Spain outside built-up areas. **2** Give way to traffic coming from the right. **3** (a) No; (b) yes; (c) no, but it is considered advisable; (d) yes; (e) no; (f) no. **4** Italy.

5 No, it would be one hour slow. 6 No, it would still be one hour slow. 7 France; no. 8 (a) Brenner; (b) Mont Cenis; (c) Simplon; (d) Great St Bernard. 9 Ireland, the Channel Islands, the Isle of Man, Malta and Gozo. 10 (a) Road works, Italian; (b) holes in the road surface, French; (c) speed limit, German; (d) accident, Dutch; (e) reverse, Portuguese; (f) right, Spanish; (g) left, German; (h) straight on, French; (i) headlamp, German; (j) gearbox, French; (k) brake, Italian; (l) tyre, Dutch. 11 Italy. 12 Australia, left; Canada, right; Cyprus, left; Greece, right; Jamaica, left; Nigeria, right; Romania, right; Sweden, right; Thailand, left; Zambia, left. 13 The Holden. 14 Makes of Chinese car: East Glows is a saloon car produced in China since 1964; East Wind, also called Dong-Feng, is the name of a number of types of Chinese vehicles produced since 1958.

Page 52 Famous competition cars

1 Mercedes-Benz 300 SLR. 2 Vauxhall 30/98 E type. 3 A.C. Cobra. 4 Lotus XI. 5 Bentley 4½ litre. 6 Porsche 917. 7 Chaparral 2E. 8 Ferrari P3. 9 Ford GT40. 10 Aston Martin DBR1/300. 11 Maserati Tipo 60 'Birdcage'. 12 Jaguar 'D' type.

Page 54 Driving and the law

1 Seventeen. 2 Driving licence, road tax licence, certificate of insurance, M.O.T. certificate if applicable. 3 70 mph. 4 30 mph. 5 Yes, if they are not working and a policeman or traffic warden waves you on. 6 Between 'lighting-up times', i.e. from half an hour after sunset to half an hour before sunrise, and in daytime in poor visibility. 7 Not if they are learning to drive a car, but heavy goods vehicle learners are. 8 Bicycles, horse-drawn vehicles, agricultural vehicles, invalid carriages and motor cycles under 50 cc. 9 Stop, except in exceptional circumstances. 10 No waiting, except for loading and unloading at times shown on nearby plates.

11 A stamp on a driving licence to show that the holder has been summonsed for a driving offence. 12 A test to determine whether a driver has been drinking. 13 When his vehicle is stationary, or in a built-up area between 11.30 p.m. and 7 a.m. 14 A test, formerly carried out by the Ministry of Transport, required by law on vehicles over three years old to test their roadworthiness. The test examines brakes, lights, steering, suspension, seat belts, tyres, wheels, windscreen wipers and washers, horn, exhaust system and silencer, and looks at the general condition of the vehicle. 15 The ability to read a car number plate (with glasses if normally worn) at 67 ft (20·4 m) for small symbols and 75 ft (22·8 m) for large symbols.

Page 55 Accessories

Hidden in the picture are: roof rack, petrol cap, oil can, exhaust silencer, manifold, wing mirror, spotlight, reversing light, windscreen wipers, de-mister, radio aerial, headrest, mud-flap, plug-spanner, jack, tow-bar ball, sliding sunroof. (See overleaf)

Page 56 The world championship

1 (a) 1950; (b) Grand Prix racing; (c) 'Nino' Farina. **2** Juan Manuel Fangio; he won the championship five times. **3** He has won more Grand Prix victories than any other driver (27). **4** Seven, in 1963. **5** Emerson Fittipaldi; 25. **6** Juan Manuel Fangio; 46. **7** One, Phil Hill. **8** (a) Jack Brabham;

(b) 1966; (c) Repco V8. **9** A McLaren M23, in Fuji, Japan, in 1976. **10** Jack Brabham. **11** N. Farina, he won the world championship in an Alfa Romeo, all the others won it in Ferraris. **12** Graham Hill, over a number of years. No-one has yet won all three in one year.

Page 58 Three-wheeler cars

1 Bond Bug. **2** Benz single cylinder 1886. **3** Berkeley T60. **4** Reliant Robin. **5** Isetta 300. **6** Heinkel. **7** BSA Scout. **8** Morgan 1927. **9** Messerschmidt.

Page 60 Road tunnels and bridges

1 The Mont Blanc tunnel is 7¼ miles (11·6 km) long. It connects France (Chamonix) with Italy (Courmayeur). **2** The Firth of Forth road bridge. **3** A bridge made from prefabricated steel sections which can be assembled quickly. This type of bridge was much used in World War II. **4** Sydney Harbour Bridge. It carries eight road lanes, two overhead electric railway tracks, a cycle track and a footway. **5** Five – Westminster, Waterloo, Blackfriars, Southwark and London. **6** Glasgow (Clyde); Liverpool (Kingsway and Queensway); London (Blackwall, Rotherhithe and Dartford). **7** A bridge where you have to pay a fee to cross. Any of the following: Batheaston, Cleddau, Clifton, Dunham, Erskine, Forth, Itchen, Middlesbrough, Penrhyndeudraeth (Briwet Bridge), Porthmadog, Selby, Severn, Shard, Swinford, Tamar, Tay, Warburton, Whitchurch and Whitney. **8** The bridge is called a pontoon. This is also the name of a card game in which the score to aim for is 21. **9** A badger run under the M5 near Exeter!

Page 61 Jargon, abbreviations and slang

1 (a) A thin painted line usually emphasising one or more lines of a car's bodywork; (b) the main bearing end of the piston connecting rod. It can also refer to the bearings where the connecting rod meets the crankshaft; (c) the amount of twisting or rotationary force produced by an engine; (d) the build-up of weight on the outside wheels of a car as it goes round a bend, causing it to lean outwards; (e) the tendency of the wheels to slide away from a corner with a forwards and sideways movement; (f) racing tyres without treads – they have special gripping qualities when heated up due to the rubber compound used in their manufacture; (g) a car with a curved sloping back which descends in a continuous line to the rear bumper; (h) a butyl-rubber mixture used to form a thick waterproof and chip-proof coating on the underside of a car; (i) to re-paint; (j) cables with 'crocodile' clip ends used to transfer power from one car's battery to another, usually to start a car which has a flat battery; (k) the checking and adjustment of a car's wheel alignment and angles; (l) small, usually triangular windows behind the sloping windscreen pillars which pivot to open; (m) the boring out of worn engine cylinders to re-shape them and allow new pistons to be fitted; (n) the de-carbonisation of the valves, combustion chambers and piston crowns of an engine. **2** (a) Engine; (b) tyres; (c) heavy-tread tyres for mud; (d) old car; (e) old-fashioned term for family saloon; (f) supercharger; (g) petrol; (h) 100 miles per hour; (i) a wrecked car; (j) rust; (k) making the tyres squeal by driving fast; (l) spinning the wheels of a dragster on a special liquid which is set alight by the friction created and thus warms the tyres to make them grip better. **3** (a) Miles per hour; (b) revolutions per minute; (c) kilometres per hour; (d) brake horse-power; (e) miles per gallon; (f) cubic centimetres, used to measure cubic capacity. **4** (a) Bonnet; (b) boot; (c) petrol; (d) silencer; (e) bumper; (f) windscreen; (g) gearchange; (h) tarmac road; (i) number plate; (j) engine; (k) to bump or nudge, e.g. when parking.

Page 62 Japanese cars

1 (a) Toyota; (b) Honda; (c) Datsun; (d) Colt Mitsubishi;

(e) Subaru; (f) Mazda. **2** (a) Toyota Crown; (b) Toyota Celica; (c) Datsun Cherry; (d) Honda Accord; (e) Subaru estate 1600; (f) Mazda 323 hatchback; (g) Colt Mitsubishi Celeste; (h) Honda Civic.

Page 64 Records

1 631·367 mph, attained by Gary Gabelich on 23rd October, 1970 in *Blue Flame*, a rocket-propelled 4-wheeled vehicle. **2** 39·245 mph; le Comte de Chasseloup-Laubat, in 1898. **3** Set a world land speed record of 121·57 mph at Daytona, Florida. **4** Sir Malcolm Campbell; nine, from 1925 to 1935. **5** (a) L. Rigolly – Gobron-Brillié; (b) M. Campbell – Sunbeam; (c) H. Segrave – Sunbeam 1000 hp; (d) J. Cobb – Railton-Mobil Special; (e) D. Campbell – Bristol-Proteus Bluebird. **6** Camille Jenatzy's *Jamais Contente* broke the land speed record in 1899 (65·79 mph) and held it for three years. **7** 268·9 mph was reached by Rudolf Caracciola on the Frankfurt Autobahn in 1938. **8** Parry Thomas's *Babs*. It broke the land speed record twice before crashing at Pendine Sands, where it was buried. **9** The world's fastest three-wheeled vehicle, driven by Craig Breedlove. **10** It was petrol driven – previous record holders were driven by electricity and steam.

Page 65 At the petrol station

1 The number of stars relates to the octane rating, so a driver can choose the one best suited to his car. **2** An air line and pressure gauge; it pumps air into tyres and measures the air pressure in them. **3** Diesel fuel – for diesel engines. **4** To check the amount of oil in the sump. **5** To top up the level in the car battery. **6** To wash car windscreens. **7** A tyre is being changed. **8** To lubricate the moving parts of the engine. **9** Yes, if the vehicle has a 2-stroke engine. **10** A second petrol tank which the car switches to when the main tank is empty. **11** A car is going through a car wash.

Page 66 Vintage cars

1 1921 Rolls Royce Silver Ghost. **2** 1922 Lancia Lambda. **3** 1922 Hispano-Suiza. **4** 1930 Austin Seven ('Tourist Trophy'). **5** 1930 Mercedes Benz type 770. **6** 1928 4½-litre Bentley. **7** 1930 Rover Light Six saloon. **8** 1923 Citroen C3 'Citron'. **9** 1929 Alfa-Romeo 6-cylinder 'Gran Sport'. **10** 1929 Bugatti type 35B.

Page 68 Motoring organisations

1 King Edward VII. **2** (a) Veteran Car Club; (b) Vintage Sports Car Club. **3** 1905. **4** Because if a patrolman did not salute a member he was giving warning of a speed trap ahead. **5** Automobile Club de l'Ouest. **6** (a) Automobile Club d'Italia (Italy); (b) Automobilclub von Deutschland (Germany); (c) Automobile Club de France (France); (d) Real Automóvil Club de España (Spain); (e) Royal Automobile Club de Belgique (Belgium); (f) Österreichischer Automobil, Motorrad und Touring Club (Austria); (g) Koninklijke Nederlandsche Automobil Club (Holland); (h) Automobil Club de Suisse (Switzerland); (i) Automóvel Club de Portugal (Portugal). **7** Institute of Advanced Motorists. **8** (a) CSI (Commission Sportive Internationale); (b) FIA (Fédération Internationale de l'Automobile). **9** Recovery service in the event of breakdown or accident; legal advice; touring service; insurance, road and weather information; engineering and technical advice; finance plans. **10** British Automobile Racing Club, British Racing Sports Car Club, British Racing Drivers Club, for which membership is by invitation only, for recognised racing drivers.

Page 69 Find your way

The black arrows indicate the shortest route.

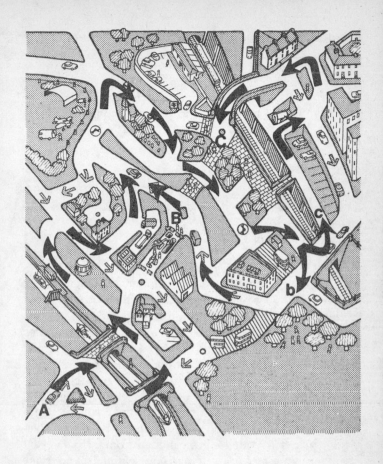

Page 70 Famous roads

1 The A1; it joins London and Edinburgh. 2 The A5. 3 (a) Edinburgh; (b) Paris; (c) Rome; (d) London; (e) Nice; (f) Brighton. 4 A Roman road that originally ran from the mouth of the River Axe in Devon to Lincoln. Modern roads follow the same route in virtually a straight line. 5 19,000 miles (30,577·5 km); it connects the Arctic Circle with the southern tip of Chile. 6 (a) The junction of the A1 and A66

115

in North Yorkshire; (b) Gravelly Hill, near Birmingham; the junction of the A38, A38(M) and the A5127; (c) a section of the A31, between Guildford and Farnham, in Surrey. 7 A road that runs along the French Riviera from Nice to Ventimiglia. 8 (a) Scotland; (b) California, USA; (c) Italy. 9 1523 miles (2451 km). It was completed in six months, between March and September 1942.

Page 71 Veteran cars

1 De Dion-Bouton 'Doctor's Coupé'. 2 Peugeot Bébé 1903. 3 Mercedes 1903. 4 Lanchester 1895. 5 Benz 4-wheel 3 hp 1900.

Page 72 Club events

1 (a) A circuit race where cars are allotted a handicap either of time or number of laps according to their proven speed or engine size; (b) a time trial on tarmac with at least one corner or chicane incorporated; (c) a time trial on a tarmac road incorporating an uphill climb; (d) a race on a circuit marked out on grass in which not more than four competitors may compete at one time; (e) a race on a circuit incorporating grass, tarmac and other surfaces; (f) a time trial from a standing start on a straight tarmac course; (g) a timed event, usually over rough country, which involves visiting places in sequence in an allocated time; (h) an event involving climbing a grass or mud course up hills and trying to get as far up as possible, with penalties awarded according to how far short of the top a competitor is; (i) a timed event on grass or tarmac involving driving forwards and in reverse, in and out of parking bays and round pylons, etc. Penalties are awarded for striking pylons or crossing forbidden areas. 2 Handicap – Anthony Blight; sprint – David Render; hillclimb – Roy Lane; autocross – John Bevan; rallycross – Rod Chapman; drag racing – Dennis Priddle;

rally – Roger Clark; sporting car trial – Jack Pearce; auto test – Trevor Smith. **3** Handicap – Talbot; sprint – Lotus 76; hillclimb – McLaren; autocross – Naveb Special; rallycross – Ford Escort RS 1800; drag racing – Mister Six; rally – Lancia Stratos; sporting car trial – Cannon; auto test – MG Midget.

Page 73 When was it made?

1 1930s – 25/30 Rolls Royce. **2** 1920s – Austin 12. **3** 1940s – Austin Cambridge. **4** 1970s – Rover 3500. **5** 1950s – Vauxhall Velox. **6** 1960s – Hillman Super Minx.

Page 74 Rallies

1 No, it is an event which combines driving and navigational skills with endurance of driver and car, though time and competition with other drivers are also important. **2** (a) Finland; (b) Greece; (c) Great Britain; (d) Kenya. **3** The Monte Carlo Rally. **4** The tulip stage (named after Holland's Tulip Rally). **5** Roger Clark, in 1972 and 1976. **6** Andrew Cowan in a Hillman Hunter in 1968. **7** A speed pilot, i.e. an instrument which shows the driver his average speed and thus lets him know if he is keeping on schedule. **8** A scale for plotting very accurate map references. **9** (a) A section of a rally which must be covered in a set time or at a given average speed; (b) the part of a rally that leads up to one or more special stages. **10** S. Munari – he is Italian, the others are all Scandinavian. **11** The Ford Escort won the World Cup Rally which ended in Mexico, and because of this Ford named this type of Escort the Escort Mexico. **12** The Safari Rally; Joghinder Singh, a Sikh garage owner, has won this rally several times in a Peugeot. **13** (a) Places that must be avoided; (b) places that must be driven through quietly; (c) un-tarmaced roads, usually single track; (d) places where drivers check in at the beginnings and ends of stages. **14** Moments when a car has four wheels in the air due to going over a bump in the road, named after the Finnish pronunciation of 'jumps'. **15** A Bean. **16** The Triumph TR7; it was the only British sports car competing in international rallying. **17** (c), The Triumph TR7, because it is the only front-engined car. The other cars are (a) Renault Alpine; (b) Lancia Stratos; (d) Porsche Carrera.

Page 76 Coachwork

1 (a) Limousine; (b) sedanca de ville; (c) cabriolet; (d) shooting brake; (e) saloon; (f) spider/spyder; (g) coupe; (h) Gran Turismo; (i) sports car. **2** Headlight, all the others are windows. **3** Just below the side or door windows. **4** A car that has no pillar dividing the front door from the back door on the same side. **5** They are all names of different kinds of rear bodywork (beetle-back, duck-tail, boat-tail, fish-tail). **6** A folding seat in the tail of a two-seater vintage car for an extra one or two passengers. **7** Governess-cart.

Page 78 Cars around the world

1 Oshawa, Acadian; **2** Windsor, Meteor; **3** São Paulo, Puma; **4** Cordoba, Torino; **5** Barcelona, Artes; **6** Leoben, Custoka; **7** Lunde, Troll; **8** Basle, Monteverdi; **9** Koprivnice, Tatra; **10** Istanbul, Anadol; **11** Haifa, Sabra; **12** Cairo, Ramses; **13** Cape Town, GSM; **14** Port Elizabeth, Ranger; **15** Uttarapara, Hindusthan; **16** Shanghai, Feng-Huang; **17** T'aipei, YLN; **18** Taren Point, Canstell; **19** Sydney, Ascort; **20** Mordialloc, Bolwell.

Page 80 More milestones

1 A twin overhead camshaft engine. It revolutionised racing car engine design. **2** They were all concepts of streamlining

118

in their own era. **3** Cadillac. **4** Citroen; the DS19 in 1955.
5 The Mini; first produced in 1959. **6** MG model M Midget.
7 It enables engines to last almost twice as long, as it does
not break down under heat. It was essential to the development of the Mini with its combined engine and gearbox.
8 (a) The Austin A40 (1958) was the first to have a '2-box'
body, and was also the first hatchback; (b) the Ford Consul
(1951) was the first to have a '3-box' body instead of having
separate wings, lights and body.

Page 82 Safety

1 (b). **2** (b). **3** Tyres, brakes, steering, lights. **4** (a), (b) and
(c). **5** MG. **6** (b). **7** (c). **8** (b). **9** (c).

Page 84 Jaguar

1 Sir William Lyons – founder of the company; 'Lofty'
England – racing chief; William Heynes – chief engineer;
Wally Hassan – engine development chief. **2** The three words
that made up Jaguar's advertising slogan for their saloon
cars. **3** Any of the following: XK120, XK140, XK150,
XKSS, C-type, D-type, E-type. **4** C-type 1951 and 1953;
D-type 1955 and 1957. **5** 1961; 151 mph (243 kph).
6 Standard Swallows. **7** XK120 – production car race, Silverstone 1949. E-type – spring meeting, Oulton Park 1961.
8 A Panther is a modern 'replica' of the SS100 using Jaguar
engine and components. **9** (a) Duncan Hamilton; (b) Ron
Flockhart; (c) Ivor Bueb; (d) Stirling Moss; (e) Tony Rolt;
(f) Roy Salvadori; (g) Masten Gregory; (h) Mike Hawthorn; (i) Paul Frère; (j) Innes Ireland. **10** All were successful racing 'specials' which used the Jaguar XK engine.
11 The Scottish racing stable that campaigned Jaguars in
the mid-Fifties, which led to their winning Le Mans in 1957.
12 1948 XK120. The design was revolutionary in its day
and considered by many to be one of the outstanding de-
signs of all time. It greatly influenced the development of

the sports car in later years. **13** Six. **14** A 12-cylinder Jaguar engine, capacity 5343 cc. **15** The Dunlop disc brake. **16** British Leyland's XJC 5·3 coupe, which competed in the European Touring Championship of 1977.

Page 86 Engine components

1 Valve. **2** Rocker. **3** Valve spring. **4** Cylinder head. **5** Push rod. **6** Dished piston. **7** Flat top piston. **8** Spark plug. **9** (a) Piston; (b) little end; (c) connecting rod; (d) big end. **10** Crankshaft. **11** (a) Clutch assembly; (b) flywheel. **12** Camshaft. **13** Starter motor. **14** Distributor (a) rotor arm; (b) points. **15** Fuel pump (mechanical type). **16** Dynamo.

Page 88 Wheels and tyres

1 Artillery wheel. **2** (a) Bugatti alloy wheel, on Bugatti type 35B; (b) Lotus 'wobbly' alloy wheel, on Lotus Eleven; (c) Alfa pressed steel wheel, on Alfa Giulietta Spider and Sprint; (d) Porsche alloy wheel, on Porsche 911 and 912; (e) Avon safety wheel, on Bristol 411 and 412; (f) Dunlop Denovo wheel and tyre, on Mini 1275 GT. **3** The Michelin tyre mascot. **4** Cross-ply tyres originally had the fabric cords running across the tyre at right angles to the direction of wheel rotation, and were later modified to run at 45° to the direction of wheel rotation. Radial tyres have fabric cords running at right angles to the direction of wheel rotation, plus a belt of fabric running around the circumference of the tyre beneath the tread. **5** By law, you must, if you mix the two types of tyre, fit radials on the back and cross-ply on the front, and you must not mix radial and cross-ply tyres on the same axle. **6** Dunlop – England; Pirelli – Italy; Semperit – Austria; Kleber – Germany; Firestone – USA; Goodyear – USA; Avon – England; Uniroyal – USA; Michelin – France. **7** Firestone, in the early 1900s. **8** Dunlop. **9** (a) Snow chains; (b) a studded tyre used for driving in snow. **10** Tyres on which the rubber has been completely replaced on the original fabric carcass.

Page 90 How far is it?

1 (a) Aberystwyth; (b) Bournemouth; (c) Cambridge; (d) Hull; (e) Leeds; (f) Norwich; (g) Shrewsbury. **2** 900 miles (1448 km). **3** (a) Amsterdam and Athens; (b) Brussels and Bucharest; (c) Lisbon and London; (d) Paris and Prague; (e) Stockholm and Stuttgart. **4** The M4, by 5 miles (8 km).

Page 91 Hatchbacks

1 Vauxhall Chevette. **2** Peugeot 104 GL. **3** Volkswagen Polo. **4** Honda Civic. **5** Fiat 127. **6** Ford Fiesta.

Page 92 True or false? Absurd facts and fancies

1 True; Charles Glidden and his wife drove a Napier 46,528 miles (74,880 km) through thirty-nine countries – Australia to the Arctic Circle, Mexico to the Middle East. **2** True; 1977 prices: Rolls Royce Camarguc £40,353, Cadillac Seville £14,888. **3** False. **4** True. **5** True; Mrs M. Hargrave failed her thirty-ninth test in eight years on 29th April, 1970, and passed the fortieth on 3rd August, 1970. **6** False. **7** True; Ben and Elinore Carslin completed the last leg of their crossing from Montreal on 24th August, 1951. **8** False. **9** True; driven by Henry Alexander. **10** True; but they later had to be removed as they did not please the authorities. **11** False. **12** True; Tazio Nuvolari did so, overtaking Varzi who had led comfortably for hundreds of kilometres in a more powerful car. **13** False. **14** True; Dick Marlow drove a Chrysler Valiant Regal automatic in reverse for 109·9 miles (176·9 km) in 4 hrs 17 mins on 30th April, 1974.

Page 94 You can fuel all of the cars some of the time . . .

1 Gas turbine, steam engine, electricity. 2 Diesel oil or methane gas, because they are more economical. 3 Any car can be converted to run on gas produced from farmyard manure. A farmer in Hampshire is reputed to have run his car on chicken manure for many years. 4 It is the first production electric car. A number were ordered by the Electricity Council. 5 50 miles (80 km). 6 All are powered by gas turbine engines. 7 Two tiny electric cars produced for use in crowded cities. 8 Howmet TX, Lotus 56 and 56B, Rover-BRM. 9 Coal gas; the container used to carry it. 10 Petrol and liquefied petroleum gas.

Air Quiz

Flying, from the early days when man first experimented with balloons to today's supersonic planes and space rockets, is the subject of this book. There are questions on aircraft and aviators, engines and airports, space and satellites. Some are easy and some will have you scratching your head, but all will provide lots of wit-testing fun. And, of course, if you are really stuck, you can check with the answers in the back.

Animal Quiz

Johnny Morris's Animal Magic television programme has been a favourite with children for fifteen years, and his knowledge and love of animals is enormous. This picture quiz book is full of all kinds of questions about animals, birds and fish, from silhouettes with zany clues to help you identify them to spot-the-difference puzzles. Some are easy and some are more difficult, but all are fun, and you will learn a lot you didn't know before as well. The book is specially suitable for readers of nine upwards, but it will provide hours of enjoyment for the whole family.

Travel Quiz

Travel Quiz is a book for all travellers, whether by train, plane, car, bus or even on foot. There are questions on all aspects of travel, including picture puzzles, recognition games, anagrams, general knowledge, geography, history, architecture, costume and food. It will provide hours of fun for the whole family, and of course all the questions are answered at the back of the book if you are stuck.

The Beaver Book of Brain Ticklers

Here are 100 puzzles and teasers to entertain, amuse and infuriate everyone between the ages of nine and ninety who enjoys a challenge. Some of the brain ticklers take the form of pictures, others you have to work out in your head – though a pencil and lots of paper will help – and some are easy, some more difficult. When you have puzzled them out you will find the answers at the back of the book and then you can try them out on your friends and relations.

Charles Booth-Jones teaches mathematics, as you might guess, and all the ticklers have been tested out on his pupils and his own family so they *can* be done – puzzle them out and don't look up the answers too soon!

More Beaver Books

We hope you have enjoyed this Beaver Book. Here are some of the other titles:

Cooking is Easy   A Beaver original. Recipes for delicious meals for every time of day, plus suggestions for special occasions, presents and eating out of doors. Written by Jane Todd, Cookery Editor for the Hamlyn Group, and illustrated by Marilyn Day and David Mostyn

The Adventures of Nicholas and the Gang   Whether they are having their photographs taken at school or playing cowboys and Indians in the garden Nicholas and his friends just can't keep out of trouble! A collection of hilarious stories by René Goscinny; illustrated by Sempé

Please Ptell Me Pterodactyl   A Beaver original. A book of monster-ous verse, describing the hilarious antics of the racing Brontosaurus, the chess-playing Yeti, Argus the 'private eye' and many other lovable monsters. Written by Charles Connell, with delightful illustrations by John Millington. For older readers

Legion of the White Tiger   An exciting tale of high adventure, set in 38 B.C., describing the hazardous journey Cerdic and Festus make to 'the land beyond the North Wind'. Written by James Watson for older readers

New Beavers are published every month and if you would like the *Beaver Bulletin* – which gives all the details – please send a large stamped addressed envelope to:

Beaver Bulletin
The Hamlyn Group
Astronaut House
Feltham
Middlesex TW14 9AR

303640